A Clinical Guide to Interpersonal Constructs and Attachment Theory

Rachel Swanick

A Clinical Guide to Interpersonal Constructs and Attachment Theory

From Theory to Application

Springer

Rachel Swanick
Music Therapy & Psychology
University of Derby
Derby, UK

ISBN 978-3-032-23727-9 ISBN 978-3-032-23728-6 (eBook)
https://doi.org/10.1007/978-3-032-23728-6

This Springer imprint is published by the registered company Springer Nature Switzerland AG
The registered company address is: Gewerbestrasse 11, 6330 Cham, Switzerland

Foreword

It is a real pleasure to see this wonderful and well-written book come to fruition and it is gratifying that Rachel Swanick has drawn on my own work, understanding and working with families and relationships from a construct theory viewpoint. She has created a coherent and deeply applicable integration of Personal Construct, Constructionist, and Attachment Theory perspectives. The Kellian approach, seeing each person as a scientist, allows the practitioner to home in sensitively to clients' specific meanings and construings in a compassionate way, which encourages a collaborative relationship between clients and the therapist. The Constructionist component enables a sensitivity to a person's socio-cultural background, and Attachment Theory allows all this to be placed in a rich developmental perspective. Swanick's writing style makes the book extremely approachable to readers from any walk of life, including people suffering from difficulties themselves. Its presentation of many usable practical tools and approaches is a tremendous resource for people working in health, social services, and education, and anyone working to help people to overcome or ameliorate life difficulties, specific disorders, and disabilities.

Visiting Professor at the University of Hertfordshire, UK Harry Procter

Competing Interests The author has no competing interests to declare that are relevant to the content of this manuscript.

Contents

Part I
An Introduction to Attachment Theory and Constructivism, Past and Present

1.1 Introduction

My journey with attachment theory started long before I had the language to explain it. I left teaching to become a music therapist as I didn't feel I could do enough for the children in my classroom. When training as a music therapist, it was the mother–baby observations and my personal therapist who showed me how to be a therapist. When my own children arrived, I had this instinct about going at their pace and keeping them close. I started my training as an APCI assessor in 2016, and I began to have the words to explain those feelings and instincts. I realised that in my therapy, or with my children, it wasn't about what we did, it was about how we did it; it was about me being really present and "there".

Since then, I have recognised how attachment theory is the golden thread running through all of our lives. Those early relationships affect our whole outlook on life. They inform, predict, and cause wonder and chaos.

The thing I love most about contemporary attachment theory, in particular, is flexibility. It has hope. We can change, and we do change. We can get something new from relationships, and we can give something new to others. I am a reformed Type A, much more able to not fix things for everyone whilst also keeping that mask of "I'm fine!". Whilst I can see some of that in my own children—you are going to really like intergenerational transmission!—I also see their security. And their security comes from my security, which came from all the people who have loved and nurtured me. My parents, best friends, husband, colleagues and those wonderful people who have let me into their attachment work. Stine Jacobsen opened the gate for me to begin my writing, assessment and training career, Pat Crittenden gave me the confidence to be bold and believe in what I do, and Harry Procter helped me fine-tune my thoughts in order to hone my craft.

Attachment theory is pro-social in its heart—we pass on what we know. So, with this book, I hope you can notice things in yourself and then have the techniques you need to help others (told you I was Type A). And, by doing this, you will add to the colourful and rich timeline in your unique way.

1.2 Acknowledgements

I always find this part the hardest to write, as I have so many people who care for me and support me, so I will keep this as brief as possible and make sure I thank you all in person.

To my husband, Mikey, and my gorgeous children, Cleo and Gabes, I love you all… you are here in between the lines on every page.

To my parents—my Mum, Steve and of course, my Dad. You all give me such different things, and you all fill my life with love.

To Kate G, thank you for your proofreading, editing, and the continuing gift of hyphens in my words.

To Davina and my students (cohorts 2024–26 and 2025–27), thank you for listening and thinking with me. I would like to say I won't start another sentence with, "Did I tell you I am writing a book?" but you know… I quite like this writing gig.

To my friends who have helped with the children, given me spaces to work, distracted me with nights out, listened to me chatter on, thank you with all of my heart (you know who you are).

And thank you to the families, students, therapists, teachers, and social workers that I have worked with over the years—and will meet in the future. This book is because of you and for you.

With my love, Rachel

Chapter 1
Attachment Theory: From Origins to the 1950s

When I hear people talking about *attachment*, they will often use the term to say how attached they are to something. You will have heard it, too, and you might use the term this way yourself. I could say that I am very attached to this laptop I'm writing on and to the green leather chair in the front room where I watch TV in the evenings. I might even say I am attached to the friendly person who works in the local shop, or I might get annoyed at my physical attachment to the door handle as I catch my cardigan pocket on it. I use these simple examples to highlight how we use the term "attachment" to describe something of which we are seemingly conscious. *Attachment theory* is something else completely. Attachment, in this sense, through the lens of attachment theory, happens whether we like it or not. It is present in all of our interactions with others across every moment of our human lives. It affects our experiences, well-being, life expectancy, and satisfaction. The aim of this book is to begin to explain why and how this happens. I am going to begin with John Bowlby and his anthropological findings, but our first, short stop-off is in quantum physics. Stay with me; it will all make sense, I promise.

In quantum physics, there is a phenomenon called quantum entanglement. In basic terms, this is the idea that when two particles collide or meet each other, they take on characteristics of each other; forever changed. Even when those particles are separated by a whole universe, they remember; their elements are entangled with each other.

Now… think of your own life and all of the people you have interacted with. So, many of those experiences and emotions from others will now be entangled with your own. Even though you may never see those people again, this imprint of feelings colours your current life, consciously and unconsciously.

This is attachment theory. With all this in your mind, let's go back to Bowlby, where it all began.

As we will note throughout our journey, attachment theory nods its head to the influence of nature—our inherent traits—and nurture—those provided in our environment and relationships. John Bowlby was born in the UK, into an

R. Swanick, *A Clinical Guide to Interpersonal Constructs and Attachment Theory*, https://doi.org/10.1007/978-3-032-23728-6_1

upper-middle-class family, where he spent a very short amount of time with his mother. At the time in this echelon of society, mothers would be with their children for only a few hours, and then the child would often attend a boarding school. When he was 4, Bowlby's Nanny died, which he described as similar to the loss of his mother (Lieneman et al., 2025). If Durant's (1926) interpretation of Aristotle's quote, "We are what we repeatedly do" (pg. 87), is correct, then we can understand Bowlby's motivations and theoretical slants as he developed attachment theory in his adult life.

Bowlby qualified as a medical doctor in 1933, and during those surrounding years, also completed his training in adult psychiatry and psychoanalysis in the UK. Ernest Jones had brought psychoanalysis to the UK in 1913, after completing his own training with Freud in Vienna. World War I curtailed the advancement of the movement in the UK and Europe. When Anna Freud and Melanie Klein found sanctuary in London, the movement took on a new energy in the psychiatric profession. Bowlby undertook his training and analysis with Klein at the same time as moving from adult psychiatry to child and family psychiatry, and it was during his work with families that Bowlby started to observe patterns that challenged both Freud's and Klein's psychoanalytic theories.

Let's look at those theories so that we have an understanding of why and how attachment theory developed. A side note: I will be using *mother and infant* in this section, as in the societal context of the late 1800s and, in fact, most of the 1900s, mothers were most often the primary caregiver. I will explore this further later in the book. Through his clinical practice, Freud noted that all humans have "innate drives"; subconscious energy that drives us to react in certain ways. These drives are there to ensure our survival, beginning in infancy and continuing throughout our lifespan. When he was observing mother–infant relationships, he saw that the infant was often satisfied by sucking (the breast or bottle) rather than being calmed by the mother. Freud thought that the oral satisfaction of the innate behaviour of sucking fulfilled the primary need of feeling safe or cared for and that the infant only learned to love their mother through association, over a longer period of time. He felt that the infant was passive in the relationship until they had developed a sense of love and attachment towards the mother (also known as the "object" in Freud's theories). Love for a caregiver was seen as the secondary effect of the infant having their primary needs (hunger in this instance) met.

Melanie Klein took Freud's theories and switched the infant's primary and secondary needs. Klein worked with psychoanalytic theories and observed children at play. Klein noted that the infant was driven to have a physical and emotional connection with the mother and that this was present from birth. Klein developed the idea of the "object" too, stating that the experience of the relationship between mother (the object) and the infant was internalised by the infant, creating a representation of all relationships for the infant. So, if the mother's object was attentive and "good", the infant would internalise this experience and know the mother would be there for them. Klein felt that infants were fantasy-driven, meaning that the infant's imagination was very active. If the infant felt pain or unhappiness, they would fantasise that the mother was bad, and when they felt happy or content, the mother/

object would be good again. In Klein's object relations theory (as set out simply here), the infant's unconscious fantasies would impact their relationships with the caregivers, for better or for worse. Any emotional problems that the infant/child/individual experienced would have been caused by the conflict in these internal fantasies and had nothing to do with the outside world. Klein had shifted the focus away from innate behaviours as set out in Freud's work to emphasising the need for emotional connection in relationships, which was and is incredibly important. Klein dismissed the impact of the external and environmental context on the development of the infant, however, and this is where Bowlby stepped in.

Bowlby began working in the London Child Guidance Clinic in 1936. As he observed and grew to know families, he noted the intense impact of the mother on the child, and vice versa. In particular, he recognised the key themes of separation, deprivation, and bereavement (loss) as having an impact on the bond between child and caregiver. Bowlby had begun to realise that the child is not an island and will certainly be influenced by the people and situations around them. In letters quoted in Ezquerro's book "Encounters with John Bowlby" (2016), we can see how Bowlby starts to question Klein's theories of being infant-centred. He talks about a patient who had a "pathogenic relationship" (pg. 19) with their mother, who had recently passed away. The patient had presented in the clinic as "anxious and agitated" (pg. 19) and as neither Bowlby or his supervisor had known about the death, they had taken a different path in treatment when perhaps they should have been working on this grief. In another vignette, Bowlby asks how we are to truly understand a person's experience of the world if we don't know about the "real-life events and situations to which he has been exposed" (pg. 19). When a three-year-old boy who presented as hyperactive and aggressive was brought to the clinic, Bowlby consulted Klein for supervision. Bowlby wanted to see the boy's mother so he could understand more fully the potential roots for the child's dysregulation. Klein, in line with her object relations theory, felt this was unnecessary and irrelevant and asked Bowlby not to do this. Bowlby followed this instruction to his chagrin and later learned that the mother had been admitted to a psychiatric facility, leaving him with a sense of having neglected the family's needs in pursuit of a pureness of theory. This moment could be seen as a turning point in the creation of Bowlby's own attachment theory.

In his clinical observations, Bowlby had discerned that many of the challenges faced by the parent and child stemmed from feelings of loss due to separation and deprivation of care. He began to offer mothers attending the clinic additional weekly meetings where they would explore the behaviours and feelings they were finding difficult. Bowlby found that mothers became "increasingly sympathetic and tolerant" (Ezquerro, 2016, pg. 23) towards the challenging behaviours as they noticed patterns within themselves, too. In 1940, Bowlby presented a controversial paper to the British Psychoanalytical Society entitled "The Influence of Early Environment in the Development of Neurosis and Neurotic Character". Bowlby shared his observations on the patterns observed in his clinic, suggesting that professionals working with children needed to be like "nurserymen"; studying the environment around the plants in order to understand their conditions and reactions fully. He discussed the impact of offering mothers' weekly meetings and began to explore what would become intergenerational attachment patterns and their effects. By using real-life observations and examples of change from mothers and their children, Bowlby encouraged professionals to move beyond internalised phantasies that concentrated solely on the child and instead to think about the child's whole context and relationships. This, as we have seen, was in direct conflict with Freud, Klein, and the foundations of the British Psychoanalytical Society at that time.

During Bowlby's time at the London Child Guidance Clinic, he also conducted observations on children who had been caught stealing during 1937–1939. At this point in history, World War II overtook the needs of medical and psychological care, and Bowlby began a role working in the Royal Army supporting the recruitment of officers alongside his family work. It wasn't therefore until 1944 that Bowlby published his next groundbreaking attachment paper, "Forty-Four Juvenile Thieves: Their Characters and Home Life". In his observations, Bowlby had compared 44 children who had been convicted of theft with 44 children in a "control group". The control group had some emotional challenges, but had not been criminally convicted. As part of the research, Bowlby categorised the children in both groups, and this provided integral information for the future creation of attachment theory as we know it. In the group who had been convicted of theft, Bowlby noted that more than a quarter were deemed "affectionless", meaning that they lacked a sense of affection or responsibility towards others. A further quarter were "constantly overactive" whilst only two children presented as "normal" or stable. It is worth reflecting that generally, the IQ of these children was above the general population, and they were mainly from financially secure families. When Bowlby compared the criminally convicted group to the control group, he found that although the main presentations of the group included depressive and anxious symptomology, there were no children who presented as "affectionless". The evidence Bowlby collected from the children's families highlighted that whilst only 5% of the control group children had experienced prolonged separation from their mothers, 40% of the convicted children had been separated from their mothers for more than 6 months, with 12 out of the 14 children who were labelled "affectionless" being part of this subsection. In interviews, mothers often reported feeling like a stranger after being reunited with their child, with some presenting as depressed or hostile towards their child. Along with possible genetic factors, having a mother who was distant either physically or emotionally became a significant factor in the correlation between children who displayed challenging behaviours and those who did not.

"Forty-Four Juvenile Thieves: Their Characters and Home Life" became a seminal moment in the creation of attachment theory. Using a strong methodological approach, Bowlby had found a causal link between the emotional quality and the level of security in the mother–child relationship, paving the way for exploration of maternal deprivation, and challenging the Psychoanalytical community by emphasising the importance of professionals understanding the whole family network. This moves from using data on actual events in the family and not solely the unconscious phantasies certainly challenged the therapeutic profession at that time. The paper became well-renowned in work with children, and led Bowlby to take an even greater career step—the publication of the 1951 WHO article on "Maternal Care and Mental Health".

*Let's take a moment here.... The next step that Bowlby took changed how people thought about families for decades, right up to the present day. At the time of writing in 2025, that is 75 years of therapeutic and social care for families, of parents shaping their own children into who they are now, of educational settings working differently. When I think about this moment as an attachment specialist myself, I look backwards and see the connections to Winnicott (*1971*), Vygotsky (*1978*), Ainsworth (*1978*), Main & Solomon (*1986*), Crittenden (*2015*), and now my own work. Those connections have grown through time like tendrils on a beautiful plant, reaching, fusing, challenging, constructing each other so that the language we use now as attachment peers is so certain and clear. Like our quantum entangling theory at the beginning of the chapter, and as Bowlby himself wanted, each attachment researcher adds another layer, another quality and colour to the theory so that as professionals we echo the foundational aspects of attachment theory around the world for the benefit of those with whom we work.*

We return to Bowlby, and it is 1951. World War II has ended, and the fallout for families is catastrophic. Men were traditionally the "breadwinners", providing financially for their wives and children. Many professions required women to stop working in this historical era, with only approximately 15% of women earning a wage in 1940. This is particularly important when thinking about attachment theory as women were (and generally remain) the main carers for children and it was the cultural norm for fathers to be absent and at work. When the Second World War began, women not only cared for their children as normal, but they were also expected to undertake paid work as men were enlisted for the armed forces. Many families were forced into being "single-parent" families during the war as a temporary state, with thousands remaining so when fathers did not return from active service. When men did return from war, their state of mind was often completely altered; divorce and separation became more prevalent. This changed social landscape saw women having to carry more of the family burden, as well as trying to find new identities in what was a new world for them. The grief and trauma they were carrying for the loss of their families led to intergenerational trauma in their children—who would have higher levels of poor health, lower education and diminished career experiences in their adult lives due to the impact of war. Children had extra layers of emotional challenge as they too carried the grief of losing a parent, of being evacuated from their homes, of not having the consistency and stimulation of education as well as the impact of financial hardship. The new societal environment created after this World War became the important context for Bowlby's WHO paper; a paper that emphasised the need to protect and support mothers specifically as they carried the heavy burden of their families.

In "Maternal Care and Mental Health", Bowlby set out his foundations of attachment theory as well as his move away from psychoanalytical technique. He rejected Freud's traditional ideas that the child has their own fully developed ego and superego, instead rightly affirming that the mother (or primary caregiver) co-regulates the child's emotional and internal states until they are mature. Bowlby wrote that the mother becomes the "psychic organiser" of the child until they are ready to do this for themselves. In his words, "*this is a slow, subtle and continuous process, beginning when he first learns to walk and feed himself, and not ending completely until maturity is reached*" (1951, pg. 53). In order for the mother/primary caregiver to provide this important co-regulation, they too need to be helped through access to financial, healthcare and social support. Bowlby specifically writes in this article, "If a community values its children it must cherish their parents" (1951, pg. 84). Without this help, Bowlby noted that there would be severe and long-term negative consequences to a child's life, further describing these phenomena as the "maternal deprivation hypothesis", symptoms of which he had observed in his previous research on the Forty-Four Juvenile Thieves (1944). Bowlby recognised the "critical period" of the first 2½ years of the child's life in the importance of establishing secure and positive connections between child and mother. This theory remains very present in contemporary child support, with the UK Government leading the "First 1000 Days" project (Parliament Publications, 2019). Again, it is Bowlby's view of the mother/primary caregiver that shows the real change in thinking. Bowlby states that for children to grow up "mentally healthy", they need "*warm and continuous care from mother or permanent mother substitute, in which both find satisfaction and enjoyment*" (1951, pg. 13). This quote emphasises two hugely important points in how we as professionals think about parenting. Firstly, although we use the term *mother* here, Bowlby is saying that it simply needs to be someone warm and consistent. Secondly, the relationship needs to be mutually satisfying—there needs to be give and take, reciprocity, shared love, and attention.

It Takes a Village…

Bowlby's main shift away from previous professional and psychoanalytical viewpoints of the child and family was that to help families, we need to think about the whole network and the context they are living within. In other words, every interaction that the child and parents have can affect them, for better or for worse. This reminded me of the West African proverb, "it takes a village to raise a child", meaning that children benefit from a diverse range of relationships to mature into well-rounded adults. For us to reach self-actualisation, we need to experience many events with different people and build resilience and knowledge from them so that we can reach our full potential. As Bowlby began to delve deeper into attachment theory, his approach to enhancing his work began to reflect the process of attachment more succinctly. By 1950, around the time of the WHO publication, Bowlby had met James Robertson and Mary Ainsworth, two key players in the village of knowledge around his "child" that is attachment theory.

Robertson began working with Bowlby in 1948 and, in fact, contributed to Bowlby's WHO paper on maternal care. Robertson was a social worker, a psychoanalyst himself, and a documentary maker—and an integral voice in the early stages of attachment theory. Robertson was deeply affected by the emotional impact of

Table 1.1 A comparison between Robertson's findings and Bowlby's findings. Author's own

Stage	Robertson	Bowlby
Protest	Cry, scream, actively search for the caregiver	Survival mechanism designed to bring the caregiver back and attract attention
Despair	Become withdrawn and quiet	Response to failure, conserving energy while the child waits for the caregiver
Detachment	Will engage with others but remain emotionally detached from parents	A defence mechanism to enable the child to survive in the absence of the caregiver, preventing them from forming new, potentially dangerous bonds with strangers

children being without their parents during hospital stays at the Tavistock and Portman NHS Trust. He felt that healthcare staff prioritised physical over emotional health and, as a result, made a poignant documentary titled, "A Two-Year Old Goes to Visit Hospital" in 1952 to highlight the effects of separation on children in clinical settings. Robertson's main contribution to attachment theory came from his observations on the separation and reunification of parents and children. The "three stages of separation distress", as we will see when we move to Mary Ainsworth, form foundational steps in our emotional understanding of attachment theory. Robertson noticed that when children were separated from their parents, they would either protest, despair, or show detachment (See Table 1.1).

With Robertson observing these patterns of separation repeatedly in children, attachment theory began to have empirical evidence for Bowlby's concept, moving the theory from abstract psychoanalytic thought to data-driven psychology. The documentaries that Robertson made highlighted tangible reactions in the children that the medical community could physically see, prompting professionals working with children to reflect and change how they thought about and worked with children in a more emotionally supportive way. For example, typically a withdrawn child might have been viewed by the medical team at the Tavistock as "setting in", but with Robertson's observations and evidence, the team could imagine that the child was actually withdrawing from the adults around them as a defence. This led to policy changes within hospitals across the UK, allowing parents to visit their children as they wished, and even moved looked-after childcare from larger institutes such as orphanages to smaller-scale foster and adoption processes. Robertson and his wife, Joyce, went on to become foster carers, leading a movement in activism for the voices and rights of children to be included in medical care.

With Robertson's important work, Bowlby was able to drive attachment theory forward again. He built on the foundation of the three stages of separation by progressing the observational behavioural focus to include a deeper, theoretical view of the evolutionary purpose of the behaviours. In the table below, we can see Robertson's observations from the parent–child separation, with the addition of *why* these behaviours happened in the context of attachment theory. This was a further step away from psychoanalytical thinking, which focused on internalised and unconscious drives, towards an ethological understanding of our biological needs.

Adding More to the Village

Mary Ainsworth began working with Bowlby and Robertson in 1950. She came from a steady middle-class background, where she was supported—and expected—to achieve highly academically. Ainsworth was closer to her father than her mother, and she was the eldest of three children. As with Bowlby, it is important to note the nurture-context Ainsworth had grown up in as we consider her enhancements to attachment theory. Ainsworth started work at the Tavistock after completing her PhD in Canada with William Blatz. Blatz developed the "security theory" in which one of the themes he posited was that children needed to develop a secure dependence on their parents before trying unfamiliar situations—another keen beginning to attachment theory. As well as this key theoretical knowledge, Ainsworth brought skills in quantitative research. For her dissertation, Ainsworth analysed autobiographical narratives with "pencil and paper" self-report scales, foreshadowing the narrative data collection which would become imperative in the development of attachment theory evidence. When Ainsworth joined the Tavistock team, she brought a huge amount of research and diagnostic experience to enable the creation of empirical data.

Ainsworth worked at the Tavistock for 4 years, initially analysing Robertson's extensive observations to create useful data. Ainsworth used her experience in narrative analysis to notate the patterns in behaviours when children were separated from their parents, further categorising potential attachment behaviours. Whilst Robertson and Ainsworth had different objectives in their work (clinical advocacy vs rigorous evidence), it was Robertson's emotional observations of the child with their family in natural situations that inspired Ainsworth's own career, which we will come to shortly.

Ainsworth's contribution to the development and use of attachment theory over many decades was far-reaching, with a pivotal moment happening when Bowlby published his WHO paper as a book in 1953. In "Child Care and the Growth of Love", Bowlby reiterated the motivating points in his original paper: consistency of care for children was imperative, the consequences of maternal deprivation on children, and advocated for "family care" over large institutions of care. In a new introduction, Bowlby also brought his initial ideas on ethology and how human parental behaviour was a reflection of animal parental behaviour. Lorenz's (1937) theory of imprinting, where ducklings would innately attach to the first object they would see, was interesting to Bowlby as he reflected on the mother–infant relationship, and also gave a theoretical framework for the instinctual attachment behaviours the observational team had gathered. Ainsworth had several criticisms of Bowlby's book. Her rigorous and systematic approach to her own work led her to feel that Bowlby's work lacked nuance and evidence. Ainsworth felt that Bowlby's definition of deprivation was too broad—leading readers unable to distinguish between the quality of care and the absence of care. Ainsworth argued that not all separations were damaging and that it was the quality of the interpersonal interactions between mother and child that had the most impact. For example, a child could have consistent care with the same parent for their entire childhood, but if the parent was affected by mental health problems or their capacity to relate to their child was affected in any way, the quality of the relationship would be damaged, with a possible negative effect on the child. Ainsworth began to develop her theory that it wasn't maternal deprivation that affected the parent–child relationship; it was the ability of the parent to be sensitive to the child's needs. Alongside the broad definitions, Ainsworth shared concerns about the lack of empirical data, with Bowlby using anecdotal evidence rather than objective and tested information. These key criticisms forced Bowlby to deepen his thinking on attachment and how data could be collected to really understand what was happening in the family dynamics. Bowlby asked, "If the disruption of a bond is important, what is the nature of the bond being disrupted?" (Stevenson-Hinde, 2007, p. 339).

By questioning and critically analysing Bowlby's work, Ainsworth had found a way to add the nuance and depth she was seeking in the theory. Counterarguments, different points of view, and theoretical bricolage are so important when we are creating theories to support humans: we have unique needs and views of the world through our experiences, and although it would be "easy" if professionals could use a one-size-fits-all technique to help families in need, this isn't possible. As we move through this book, we will see how the next researcher or theoretician brought more nuance and depth to attachment theory. For attachment theory to be really useful for families, we needed to bring the individual sensitivity that Ainsworth was suggesting into professional work.... But I am jumping ahead. We still have a lot of foundations to lay...

As Bowlby moved away from traditional psychoanalysis, he sought a new theoretical framework in which to anchor his burgeoning theory. It was in the work of Konrad Lorenz (1937) and in Ethology that Bowlby found echoes of his own observations and ideas. Lorenz, an Austrian zoologist and ethologist, identified behaviours in animals that indicated an emphasis on genetics and natural instincts, rather than behaviours learned from their social surroundings. This was in contrast to contemporary American behavioural psychology, and in fact sparked the decades-long debate of whether nature or nurture had the most impact on human development. Behaviourists view animals and humans as "tabula rasa", inferring that all behaviours are only learned through environmental and reciprocal action. This could be through what is known as "classical conditioning", the association of two stimuli as in the theory of Pavlov's dog, or "operant conditioning", learning rewards and punishments through consequence of action (1927). Lorenz argued that actually some behaviours were "hard wired" (1937) and used by animals and humans to create safety and longevity of their species. He noted that instead of behavioural theory being something that was universal to all, instinctual and genetic behaviours were, in fact, species-specific, biologically designed to ensure the survival of their lineage. In this, Bowlby found echoes he needed for attachment theory and began to correspond and even observe Lorenz's experimental work closely.

Lorenz had observed what he called "imprinting" in goslings, where they would become attached to the first object they saw after being born—animal, human, or other. This "critical period" (1937) in attachment development attracted Bowlby as he had observed what he thought were similar patterns in attachment behaviour between mother and infant. Whilst Lorenz was absolute in his description of intuitive behaviours, Bowlby had some flexibility of thought, expressing that the "critical period" in humans was the first 2½ years of life. During that time, it was imperative for a healthy attachment to be formed for the infant to develop well into childhood. If the infant did not form a positive attachment at this point, Bowlby suggested that this would lead to "permanent damage", meaning that the child was either attached or not attached going forward.

Here we return to Ainsworth, who questioned Bowlby's assumptions based on her own evidential observations. In her own work, Ainsworth had seen a wider flexibility of attachment between parent and infant, noting that there was a much more varied spectrum of interpersonal relationships beyond attached or not attached. With this variety, Ainsworth revealed a "sensitive period" rather than a critical period, highlighting that although these early years of development were important, attachment behaviours could be modified later in life. Perhaps the most significant challenge from Ainsworth, especially as we progress across the development of attachment theory, was that attachment behaviours were not species-specific as both Lorenz and Bowlby had found, they were actually individualised, depending on the emotional and physical context of the child. With Ainsworth being an empiricist researcher, she left the Tavistock in 1953, moving to Uganda to study mother–infant relationships in a new context.

Ainsworth's husband was offered a research position in Uganda, and, as Ainsworth had been convinced by Robertson's naturalist observations of families, and as she was curious as to the universal validity of Bowlby and the team's attachment findings, she undertook her first independent study in East Africa.

Between 1954 and 1955, Ainsworth observed 28 mothers with pre-weaned infants (1–24 months) for 2 h, every 2 weeks over 9 months. Her findings convinced her of Bowlby's ethological stance; commonly, infants showed a preferential interest towards their mother (or main caregiver), with mother and infant showing proximity-promoting signals and behaviours (1978). Ainsworth combined her knowledge gained from working with Blatz's security theory with Bowlby's ideas on maternal deprivation to understand the concept of emotional security on a deeper level. Most importantly, she found that a mother's sensitivity and responsiveness—regardless of cultural variations in Uganda and the UK—would predict an infant's feelings of potential security in attachment. The data Ainsworth collected in Uganda remained dormant until 1967, as she returned to the USA to take a teaching role. However, Ainsworth and Bowlby began a "lifelong correspondence of letters" during these years, sharing and influencing each other's views on attachment theory from afar. It was in the following years that many influential articles were written, together and separately, on their attachment theories, building the shape of the theory to what we know in the present day.

Having traced Bowlby and Ainsworth's theoretical journey and the intellectual climate in which attachment theory emerged, it is helpful to pause and consider the key empirical and theoretical papers that consolidated Bowlby's thinking. The following articles mark pivotal moments in the formalisation of attachment theory, each extending the model beyond infancy, challenging prevailing psychoanalytic assumptions, and foregrounding the lifelong impact of early relational experience. Together, they illustrate Bowlby's gradual shift from observation to theory building, as well as the controversy his ideas provoked within the psychoanalytic establishment.

In "The Effects of Mother-Child Separation: A Follow-up Study" (Ainsworth et al., 1956), the research team reviewed their attachment theory work so far and began to link attachment development to the whole human lifespan. As we have read above, Bowlby and the team had noted over many observations the potentially derogative effect that separations from the mother can have on children. The article describes how psychoanalytical theory states that for adults to experience "healthy" relationships, they need to have had stable and consistent care from a "love object" in the first 3–5 years of life. The sample for the study consisted of 60 children who had been in a sanatorium for tuberculosis before the age of 4, with children being separated from their parents between 0 and 24+ months (the majority of children had been in the sanatorium between 6 and 23 months). Reports from teachers and psychologists highlighted that when compared to children of more natural development (without separations), the children in the research group showed more difficulties in their learning and social relationships. Observations detailed children who were either withdrawn and "cold", in excessive need of their parents' attention, or ambivalent and hostile. Bowlby and the team felt that a withdrawn child was the most "serious" of all. The wider profession questioned the research team's findings, suggesting that the data were debatable due to a lack of proper control groups, a reliance on retrospective information from parents, and too much emphasis on correlational data (a link between separation issues and later issues, for example). However, this mixed-methods study sparked energy in the psychological profession, with many professionals undertaking research this way, initially to challenge and/or confirm Bowlby's team's findings.

"The Nature of the Child's Tie to his Mother" (Bowlby, 1958) was published in the International Journal of Psychoanalysis and set out Bowlby's theory with an emphasis on moving away from psychoanalytical thought. In the article, Bowlby rejected the traditional idea that the motivation of the infant's attachment was "libidinal" and instead followed his enquiry into ethology. Bowlby stated that infants were created by "Nature [to] beguile and enslave their mothers" (1958) to ensure their own survival. The proximity-seeking behaviours of sucking, crying, smiling, clinging, and following (with the latter two being the most important in his view) all had the aim of activating responsive feelings in the mother to protect the child. He offered that the mother–infant dyad was a "biological system in itself (Vicedo, 2011). In this system, the infants' behaviours, or "social releasers", are responded to by the "caregiver response", creating a feedback cycle which combines cognitive and physical actions. Bowlby noted that the pattern of interaction in this caregiving system was present across the lifespan of the dyad. This was a paramount observation, as most theorists up until this point had concentrated on those early mother–infant responses as episodically developmental.

In 1960a, Bowlby published "Separation Anxiety". This article is built on the work presented by Robertson's research on the detrimental effects of separation between child and parent. Bowlby presented Robertson's three phases of separation (see Table 1.1) and explained that a child experiences separation anxiety when a situation activates both "separation and attachment behaviours" without an attachment figure to regulate them. In a further step away from traditional psychoanalytical thought and one closer to the formulation of attachment theory, Bowlby challenged Freud's concept of overindulgence. This concept proposes that if an infant is "overly gratified" during their development, they will become dependent, passive, and resistant to growth in adulthood. Bowlby felt that what professionals needed to do instead was to understand the impact of the parents' own experiences, past and present, so that the parents could have more capacity to attend to the child's needs. Here we see the seed being planted for the many decades coming where we, parents and professionals, began to think about meeting the child's needs first so that they develop fully—keep this in your mind for later. A key element of the separation anxiety publication was that Bowlby noted that there are times when this anxiety is not present, and this is when we should worry. As we saw in Robertson's work, having an "easy" child who does not protest and is deemed as mature could actually be an intense emotional withdrawal in the child, something which needs to be thought about by the adults around them.

The final article in this was deemed as perhaps the most controversial—"Grief and mourning in infancy and early childhood" (Bowlby, 1960b). In the article, Bowlby argued that grief and mourning appear in infant and child behaviour whenever there is a disruption in their attachment relationships. If the child experiences many disruptions, then this would have a negative effect on the child's interpersonal relationships as they develop. Bowlby used observations gathered by Robertson again to notate the process of grief in children—moving from protest to despair to detachment. Later, Bowlby would emphasise that grief is a process and not a state, and something humans progress through.

Bowlby's standpoint on grief challenged the psychoanalytic community deeply, more so than the previous articles he had published. Anna Freud, a prominent member of the British Psychoanalytical Society and daughter of Sigmund, strongly contended the article. Freud stated that infants could not experience bereavement as they had insufficient ego development and that they would only suffer bouts of separation anxiety with a substitute caregiver. Spitz, another member of the society asked fellow Psychoanalysts to not "rock the boat" and challenge psychoanalysis too much. As a result of this interaction, Bowlby became a silent member of the BPS, refusing to discuss his work there any further.

As we finish this chapter, I will acknowledge that there was so much more I could add here about the beginnings of attachment theory and Bowlby's spark of energy that motivated others. As we move into the next chapter, which will bring us up to contemporary attachment theory, there will be overlaps and returns to the foundations of the work. Below is the timeline of our theoretical journey so far.

Attachment theory development timeline		
Early 1900s	Freud's Cupboard Love	Dominant psychoanalytic view: attachment is a learned, secondary drive based on food provision and pleasure.
1920s–1940s	Klein's object relations	Influential psychoanalytic theory focusing on the infant's internal world of fantasies about "objects"
1930s	Bowlby begins at the Tavistock Blatz's security theory	John Bowlby observes the link between maternal loss and later delinquency. William Blatz develops "security theory", influencing Ainsworth's focus on secure dependence as a base for exploration
1944	Bowlby's Forty-Four Juvenile Thieves Study	Links early, prolonged maternal separation to the development of an "affectionless character"
1948	Bowlby and Robertson begin work together	Bowlby sets up the Separation Research Unit and hires James Robertson to conduct observational studies.
1950s	Bowlby's exploration of ethology	Using key theories and concepts from Lorenz to provide a foundation for attachment theory
1951	Bowlby's WHO report	Puts forth the maternal deprivation hypothesis, arguing that continuous maternal care is vital for mental health.
1952	Robertson's film	*A Two-Year-Old Goes to Hospital* is released, dramatically showing the distress of separation and influencing hospital policies.
1954	Ainsworth's Ugandan study	Ainsworth moves to Uganda and begins her first independent field study, observing mother-infant interactions naturally and gathering empirical data for her sensitivity hypothesis.
1956–1960	Key articles released	Attachment theory begins to take shape and is addressed to a wider audience. "The Effects of Mother-Child Separation: a Follow-up Study", "The Nature of the Child's Tie to his Mother", "Separation Anxiety", and "Grief and Mourning in Infancy and Early Childhood" bring together Bowlby and Ainsworth's theories

Chapter 2
Contemporary Attachment Theory

We return to our story of attachment in 1967. Culturally, there was a huge shift across the Western World with the 1950s being characterised by post-war recovery and the move into the 1960s being coloured by more affluence, pop culture and a greater sense of permissiveness. The role of women was challenged in society; many women were able to focus on careers and have access to contraception. Female authors wrote leading texts on female experiences at this time. This is important to think about in our attachment journey, as the next clinical and research steps were taken by women. So far in the creation of attachment theory, there had been Bowlby, Blatz, and Robertson, to name the key male figures. Now, Ainsworth was ready to take centre-stage with her robust use of qualitative observations and quantitative research methods.

Ainsworth published her findings from the Ugandan study in 1967. It is interesting to note both that it had taken many years for her to share her data and how it also provided an energy shift for Ainsworth, as it would inform her work and career for the coming decades. In the publication, Ainsworth discussed the importance of her cross-cultural study, beginning to formalise ideas around the types of behaviours mothers shared across continents, how mothers responded in different ways to infants with different effects and ideas on the need to provide a secure base from which infants develop.

Ainsworth took these experiences and theories and began a study in Baltimore, USA, which included 26 mother–infant dyads being observed from birth to 12 months old. The aim of the study was to confirm or challenge the findings that Ainsworth had seen in Uganda and also Bowlby's theoretical foundations. Ainsworth had a team of researchers who would conduct monthly home visits to gather narrative records on the interactions between mother and infant. On average, 72 h of observations were collected (Ainsworth, 1967). When the infant was 12 months old, the dyads participated in an assessment called the "strange situation procedure".

The strange situation procedure (SSP) is arguably the most important element in the advancement of attachment theory. Bowlby had created a solid theoretical

R. Swanick, *A Clinical Guide to Interpersonal Constructs and Attachment Theory*, https://doi.org/10.1007/978-3-032-23728-6_2

framework (with the support of Robertson and Ainsworth, amongst others), and now Ainsworth provided an opportunity for researchers to empirically test attachment theory, moving it further away from traditional psychoanalysis to data-driven science. The SSP is a "standardised controlled observational method" created to understand the behaviours presented by the infant in relation to their caregiver. The SSP takes place, usually, in a clinic or laboratory, with researchers observing the session through two-way mirrors. The primary aim of the SSP is to activate the infant's attachment systems through mild stress to observe how they respond to their caregiver. There are eight stages, or tasks, detailed below, in the SSP, and the whole session lasts around 20 min. The researchers observed the interactions with four key behaviours in mind (Table 2.1).

With the data collection, Ainsworth was able to categorise a set of standard behaviours relating to three attachment styles in infants (Table 2.2, below).

We can now compare the progression of attachment theory through the categorisation of the behaviours, from Robertson to Bowlby to Ainsworth (Table 2.3).

This important shift in attachment classification brought nuance to the descriptions of attachment patterns in infant behaviour, whilst also highlighting that positive attachment patterns can and do happen (the addition of "secure"). In this initial study, Ainsworth found that 70% of the study population displayed secure attachment patterns, whilst both insecure types related to 15% each of the study population. Since this study was published, it has been repeated many times, giving similar results and emphasising the "gold standard" of predictive validity in this technique for assessing attachment patterns.

A further key progression in attachment theory occurred in Ainsworth's new ideas on maternal sensitivity. Through the many years of clinical observation, Ainsworth had seen how mothers interacted with their children and how this affected the child. We see, again, a progression of previous Bowlby theories. Bowlby had discussed how long separations and absences from mothers affected children in

Table 2.1 Detailed description of the eight stages of the Strange Situation Procedure. Author's own

The eight stages in the strange situation procedure	Four key behaviour classifications
Stage 1—Caregiver and child enter the playroom *Stage 2*—The child is encouraged to explore *Stage 3*—Stranger enters and attempts to interact *Stage 4*—Caregiver leaves while the stranger is present *Stage 5*—Caregiver enters and the stranger leaves *Stage 6*—Caregiver leaves *Stage 7*—Stranger returns *Stage 8*—Caregiver returns and interacts with the child	• *Exploration*—Is the infant interested in exploring the environment? • *Separation anxiety*—Does the infant show they are distressed when the caregiver leaves, and how? • *Stranger anxiety*—How does the infant react to the stranger in the room? • *Reunion behaviour*—How does the infant respond when the caregiver returns?

Table 2.2 Ainsworth's categorisation of attachment behaviours. Author's own

Attachment category	Behaviours
Secure (Type B)	Infants use their caregiver as a secure base for exploration and are easily comforted on reunion
Insecure-avoidant (Type A)	Infants show little distress upon separation and actively avoid the caregiver on reunion
Insecure-resistant (Type C)	Infants were highly distressed by separation but resisted the caregiver's attempts of comfort in reunion

Table 2.3 Comparison table on the progression of attachment theory from Robertson, Bowlby, and Ainsworth. Author's own

Stage	Robertson	Bowlby	Ainsworth
Protest	Cry, scream, actively search for the caregiver	Survival mechanism designed to bring the caregiver back and attract attention	Insecure-resistant (Type C)
Despair	Become withdrawn and quiet	Response to failure, conserving energy while the child waits for the caregiver	Insecure-avoidant (Type A)
Detachment	Will engage with others but remain emotionally detached from parents	A defence mechanism to enable the child to survive in the absence of the caregiver, preventing them from forming new, potentially dangerous bonds with strangers	Insecure-resistant (Type C)
N/A	N/A	N/A	Secure (Type B)

long-term negative ways through his theory of maternal deprivation (Bowlby, 1953). Ainsworth's observations had led her instead to believe it was the *quality* of the interactions between mother and child that had the greatest impact, and, being the rigorous researcher, she wanted to find a way to measure and prove this. The SSP provided the clinical and technical setting to achieve this. With the aim of the protocol being to activate the infant's attachment behaviours and observe how the mother responds, Ainsworth now had the data to analyse. For example, when infants were categorised as showing secure attachment behaviours, it was noted that their mothers were appropriately responsive and sensitive to their infants, providing comfort and space as needed. When infants presented with insecure attachment behaviours, rejecting or withdrawing from their mother, the mothers showed similar behaviours towards the child. In the SSP sessions, Ainsworth saw the maternal behaviours she had noted in her previous projects and was able to give her observations and feelings concrete names through the categorisation of each recorded interaction. Through the SSP, Ainsworth had shown the wider clinical profession not only the importance of using empirical evidence but also that data collection was possible and meaningful when trying to capture emotive and psychological information in clients (Table 2.4).

We have one more major addition in Bowlby's and Ainsworth's theories to think about: Internal Working Models (IWM), a term first coined by Kenneth Craik

Table 2.4 Ainsworth's key observations in maternal sensitivity. Author's own

Ainsworth's key observations in maternal Sensitivity	
Awareness	The caregiver notices the infant's signals—crying, smiling, reaching out, etc.
Accurate interpretation	The caregiver correctly interprets what the infant needs—crying for food rather than sleep, for example.
Appropriate responsiveness	The caregiver's response matches the infant's needs—comfort when crying, for example.
Prompt responsiveness	The caregiver responds in a timely way—appropriate to the child's age and level of need.

(1943), and an integral theory in our journey to contemporary attachment theory. Craik had proposed that we carry "small-scale models" (1943) of our reality internally so that we can predict or refute how others around us will act. The function of these internal models is to use these predictions, which are based on previous experiences, to keep ourselves physically and emotionally safe. To quote Craik, "[we] try out various alternatives, conclude which is the best of them, [and] react to future situations before they arise" (1943, pg. 61). Working together, Ainsworth provided the empirical evidence for Bowlby's extension of this theory in his 1969 book, "Attachment".

According to Bowlby, our IWM provides a "blueprint" for how we do and will react in interpersonal relationships throughout our whole lives. Our blueprint is created in those early parent–child interactions and (depending on how those relationships were experienced) will affect our attachment behaviours in the future. If a child has a responsive and sensitive parent who meets their needs at the right time, the child will grow an internal working model that predicts that other people can be relied upon and are safe. Conversely, if a child has experienced a parent who is very anxious and does not help the child when in need, the child's internal working model will predict that when they ask for support in the future, others will not help them. This results in the grown child perhaps not asking for help and being overindependent and/or experiencing high levels of anxiety. In Bowlby's theory, IWM supports the individual to feel safe. The IWM offers a guide for us to navigate social interactions and ensure our survival on a very basic level as we seek proximity to those whose behaviours we can predict. A note on behaviours and IWM—both of these elements (and in fact all attachment behavioural associations) can be maladaptive or adaptive in what is a move away from the conventional language of "positive" and "negative" behaviours. When a behaviour is adaptive, it is something that an individual will use to keep themselves safe in that context. This could be people pleasing to appease a dominating parent, or siblings being overly aggressive with each other to keep their space in the home. It can also be secure behaviours, too, for example, feeling content in home or school. When those adaptive behaviours are taken out of the context, they become maladaptive. When a child who is aggressive in the home takes those behaviours into school (a different context), the adaptive behaviours (those which have kept them safe in the home) become maladaptive as they are not appropriate in the next context. The same is true for secure behaviours.

When a child takes their expectation that adults can be relied upon from home into a school where teachers may not be responsive, the adaptive behaviours from home become maladaptive in school, as they do not keep the child safe—even though we would like children to express a positive expectation of adults. Bowlby found that the IWM remains mostly stable throughout life unless there is a therapeutic or emotional intervention which brings a different awareness to the individual. This means that those early life interpersonal experiences in the parent dyad become integral to all of our relationships throughout life, be that friendship, romance, work or our own parenting.

The Internal Working Model (IWM) is an overarching network to explain how we store relational information that affects our external behaviours. Within the IWM, we have a set of cognitive systems that interact with each other, adding nuanced information to create those external behaviours. This complex network receives external stimuli through human interactions or sensory and situational information, processes the need in that moment and decides which elements of the system need to be activated—much like a pre-programmed computer. The systems are activated or deactivated based on the goal of that system (more on this below), and those blueprint memories are stored from early childhood onwards. The systems, therefore, inform our beliefs, attitudes, and expectations of the world around us so that we can keep safe (Fig. 2.1).

The attachment system is generally deactivated. When an individual feels distress through pain, fear, or separation from their caregiver, the system is activated. This means the individual will display their personal attachment behaviours, such as crying, smiling, and reaching out, to try to gain the attention of their caregiver. Once those needs have been acknowledged, the system calms and is deactivated again. The goal of the attachment system is to maintain proximity to a caregiver to help the individual feel emotionally and physically safe.

The caregiving system is based on Ainsworth's theory of maternal sensitivity and interlocks with the attachment system. When an individual's attachment system is activated, and there is another person there to respond, the caregiving system is activated in the second person with the goal of keeping the vulnerable person safe. This will happen between parent and infant, and also across the whole human lifespan. When this works well, the caregiver is emotionally responsive, may provide physical contact and is consistent and reliable. Once the vulnerable person's attachment system is deactivated, so too will the caregiving system be deactivated.

The exploratory system is activated when there is a new interest for the individual. The aim of the system is to support the individual to "figure things out" through

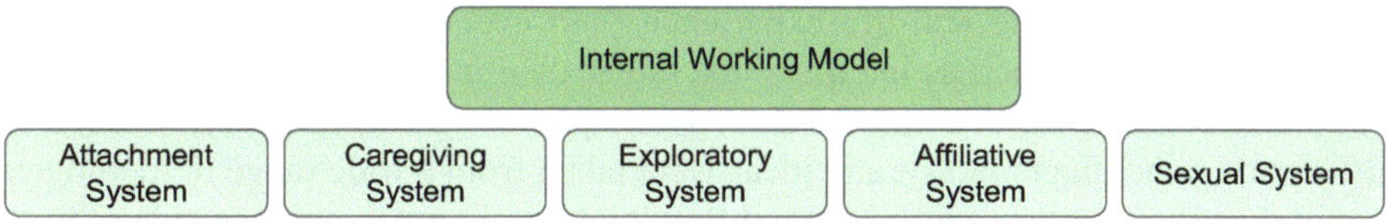

Fig. 2.1 Description of internal working systems. Author's own

play and physical interaction. This could be through imaginative play in infants and through hobbies and creative pursuits in adulthood. This system is said to have an antagonistic relationship to the attachment system, as the exploratory system is only active when the attachment system is deactivated. To explain, humans have to feel safe in order to play and explore. We have to be able to switch off our hypervigilant brains so that we can immerse ourselves in something unfamiliar, something that we might not be very good at, where failure and repairs may be needed. In those moments, our attachment system is switched off, too. If we start to feel unsafe, our safety needs change, and the attachment system becomes activated, deactivating the exploratory system as we seek familiarity over the unfamiliar.

The affiliative system develops later in childhood and is an evolutionary system which helps us to integrate into larger groups (school, community, etc.). Whilst the attachment system is similar in that it encourages humans to connect with others, the attachment system focuses on individual caregivers, and the affiliative system supports broader connections. When working well, this enables humans to share resources such as food, finances, or to problem-solve, and helps reduce stress in individuals as we develop prosocial skills. This system is active when we desire the company of others in social occasions, and we feel safe. This system is in opposition to the attachment system, so it is only active when the attachment system is deactivated. The affiliative system works with the attachment, the caregiving, and the sexual systems.

The sexual system works alongside the attachment and caregiving systems so that we can form meaningful relationships to reproduce in adulthood. On a biological level, the sexual system is integral to the longevity of the human race. The behaviours associated with this system—kissing, cuddling, physical contact—are also present in the caregiving system and activated by the attachment system. This system also promotes positive bonding in parents, with the bodily chemicals released after birth there to keep parents together to protect their vulnerable infant.

The late 1960s brought the publication of Ainsworth's Strange Situation Procedure (Ainsworth & Bell, 1970) and Bowlby's Attachment Loss Trilogy (1967–1970), bringing to attachment theory a strong foundational base on which professionals could build their practice with children and families. Ainsworth's publication became the "gold standard" for identifying the three types of attachment, whilst Bowlby's papers cemented the behavioural, evolutionary and psychological effects of attachment relationships in families. Ainsworth and Bowlby were working alongside each other to create a bricolaged theoretical underpinning for contemporary family therapy and support. I realise we have already discussed the move away from traditional psychoanalytical theory, but with these key publications entering circulation, we are only left with shadows of this older viewpoint. Now there was focus on the real-life experiences and events of families; behavioural motivations were framed as interpersonal rather than instinctual, qualitative observations were backed with empirical data, psychopathology was formed from adverse life events rather than fantasy, and ideas were taken from a wide range of ideologies rather than the singular. Ainsworth and Bowlby brought out the human side of family work, highlighting the unique experiences of each family, which were affected by not only the nature side of genetics and heritage but also, in a nurture sense, by thinking about the family in their particular bio-psycho-social context. The world around the families and researchers was changing too, and it is always important for professionals to move with societal changes. By 1970, the Equal Pay Act in the UK came into force, enabling women to take employment. Alongside this, there was a "divorce revolution", doubling the number of divorces between 1960 and 1970. Men were also questioning their place in the home and society as male unemployment rose and there was a financial crisis globally. This huge shift affected millions of children as individual parents, and parents collectively, became the first people in their families to work, not work, or face these unique struggles. As we know with attachment patterns and IWM, parental sensitivity and capacity impact on the child. Children were more often being cared for by more than one person—this was a change in Western cultures. Divorced parents were sharing childcare, children were more likely to be in childcare or daycare, and many families were under deep financial stress, either through family changes or due to the financial crisis. Attachment researchers noticed changes in the coping strategies of children as they tried to navigate the psychological changes, sometimes without the words to express their feelings. It was noted that children were using more "adaptive" functional behaviours such as masking their feelings or increased aggressive behaviours in different childcare settings due to the perceived stress and strain. Bowlby said at the start of our journey that he wanted others to add to the advancement of attachment theory, so with all this in mind, our next important person steps in—Mary Main.

Mary Main has been described as a "remarkable" psychologist who provided a "revolutionary" shift in attachment theory through her research (Van IJzendoorn, & Bakermans-Kranenburg, 1997; Duschinsky, 2024). Main's childhood was challenging as her father returned from war addicted to amphetamines and would experience psychotic episodes throughout Main's own early developmental time. She experienced chronic health problems in later life as well as depressive episodes, which she felt were related to her childhood experiences. Main acknowledged that her nurture context motivated her professional work in both positive and detrimental ways. Main was a protege of Ainsworth, belonging to the first group of graduates under Ainsworth's teaching in the 1960s. Main took a role at the University of California in 1973 and remained there for many years. She experienced significant gender bias as the first female colleague in the department for 47 years (Duschinsky, 2024). With all of these obstacles in the way of her potential progression, it is a testament to Main's resilience and focus that she went on to lead "Phase 2" of attachment theory.

Whilst Bowlby and Ainsworth's "Phase 1" had concentrated on building evidence from observational materials, Phase 2 of attachment theory concentrated on the internal processes of humans and how this affected their relationships and life experience. In the early 1980s, Main invited families to return to take part in the strange situation procedure (SSP) as part of the Berkeley Social Development Study. The families had originally taken part in the study 6 years earlier, when their children were infants, and Main wanted to assess their attachment development as part of a longitudinal study. This study was a further step in the development of the theory as it included mothers and fathers, and excluded children who were in day-care 25 h/week—a new condition due to the social changes in the world. Main recruited 189 families in total, and 92 were finally analysed with the help of Donna Weston (Main & Weston, 1981). To recap on the SSP, there are eight stages to the procedure, with one containing a reunification between child and caregiver. The research observers note how the child responds to the reunification, and this behavioural information is cross-referenced against Ainsworth's attachment categories. However, the research team noticed that this time around, 10% of the children were displaying behaviours not observed or recorded in Ainsworth's three attachment categories. These children were confused, apprehensive and even conflicted at the return of their caregiver, sometimes freezing or becoming aggressive. Main consulted the foundational theories of attachment theory and ethology, finding that in Bowlby's Attachment book (1969), he had stated that when two or more internal behavioural systems become activated (see IWM above), the cognitive conflict caused presents in conflicted physical signs such as seeking comfort and rejecting the comfort simultaneously. Main also consulted colleagues, and it was in fact Judith Solomon who had observed a fourth attachment category in the late 1970s, writing about the observed behaviours that, "it was not Type A and it is not B and it is not C. I'm going to call it D" (Duschensky, 2024). That more than one researcher had identified these behaviours motivated Main to solidify the classification, naming Type D attachment behaviours as "disorganised".

Main became curious about the parents of the "disorganised" children and questioned the nature-nurture elements of the presenting behaviours. Main worked with the psychologists Carol George and Nancy Kaplan to create a semi-structured interview for parents about their own childhoods. They applied a "cover and guess" method where they would interview parents, analyse the information collected to predict the attachment behaviours of the child and then assess the child to confirm or reject their hypothesis. This helped to identify behavioural traits in children with parental experiences. The research team deepened their understanding when they started to think about not only "what" the parents said, but "how" they said it, listening and observing vocal tones, gestures and body language. Main drew on the philosopher H. Paul Grice's Maxims of Conversation (Quality, Quantity, Relation, and Manner) to evaluate the coherence of the parents' narrative. The foundation of this theory is that individuals must use truthfulness with the right levels of information, relevance and clarity to co-operate with each other to be understood. This led to Main's semi-structured interview becoming the structured and empirically evidenced Adult Attachment Interview (AAI).

The AAI consists of 20 questions aimed at "surprising the unconscious to 'reveal itself'" (Duschinsky, 2025). As stated above, the questionnaire is not scored based on what the interviewee shares but on how they say it, with adjectives and emotive responses being analysed by the interviewer. For example, when an individual talks about the death of a parent, do they describe their grief as something resolved or a present feeling? When talking about a difficult experience, does the person use language that suggests they are still feeling the pain, or do they wash over what happened, perhaps saying it was "nothing". By thinking about the feelings behind the language as well as the use of adjectives and tenses, the researchers would gain information on how the individual coped with situations (did they ask for help, mask it, become aggressive, etc.) and relate this to their behaviours as parents. These coping techniques and behaviours would then be used to predict the behaviours of the children related to their parents. For example—and I am simplifying here—when the child was upset, would they ask for help, pretend everything was okay, or become aggressive? Through these observations, the researchers made one of the most important discoveries in psychology—that attachment behaviours could be intergenerationally transmitted. This means that if a parent avoids talking about heavy feelings, then so will the child because that is what they have been taught. If a parent manages anger with aggressive outbursts, then so too will the child. If a parent asks for help and provides comfort to others, then the child will mirror this. "*We are what we repeatedly do*"; I often come back to this phrase in attachment theory. Sometimes it feels negative; I can only act in this way because that is all I know. But mainly, it feels positive. I can change what I do as long as I do it repeatedly, as long as I live it. Intergenerational transmission is the theoretical underpinning of this short quote, and as we progress through this book, we will return and understand more deeply why this happens. At this point in our attachment story, we must acknowledge the breakthrough that the discovery meant to the progression of attachment theory. Now that researchers and professionals could almost predict how children were going to behave based on parental behaviours, they could begin to target those "at risk" in order to provide focused support. If we jump forward to 2025, research (Kaur & Bekes, 2025) is still being undertaken into just how imperative the understanding of intergenerational transmission is in building reflexive and meaningful healthcare for families.

The AAI provided another breakthrough for attachment theory by providing clear evidence for disorganised attachment. The behaviours shown by children in this heavily dysregulated state provided information on how maltreatment and abuse affected children. Many times, the children observed would present as if scared, and the observers noted that there would be no stimulus to cause the reaction. The parents who were connected to these children would have shown high levels of unresolved trauma, loss and maltreatment for themselves, passing these feelings on to their child through intergenerational transmissions. I think of disorganised attachment behaviours as a literal definition. It can feel like the brain and body have become disorganised, like they are falling apart. With secure and insecure patterns, there are coping mechanisms available to organise the self into safety; there are boundaries of some description. In disorganised patterns, there are no boundaries or safety-seeking, and it can feel distressing for the individual as well as the people around them. These are the people for whom society often has no hope and the people about whom we as clinicians worry most.

The table below details the definitions of the four attachment patterns and their connected behaviours (Table 2.5).

The social implications of the creation of the AAI were vast. Professionals now had an evidence assessment tool for both parent and child—the AAI and the SSP—which could provide vital information on how they were functioning together and,

Table 2.5 Behaviours observed in the adult attachment interviews

Attachment pattern	Behaviours observed in AAI
Autonomous (secure)	Narratives are coherent and balanced. The speaker values attachment but remains objective about their parents.
Dismissing (insecure-avoidant)	Narratives often normalise or "gloss over" negative experiences. Speakers may claim they can't remember much or provide "glorified" adjectives without supporting memories.
Preoccupied (insecure-resistant)	Narratives are often long, rambling, and filled with current anger or passive confusion. The speaker seems still "caught up" in their past relationship with their parents.
Unresolved/ disorganised	This special category is for individuals who show lapses in reasoning or discourse, specifically when discussing loss or trauma (e.g. speaking as if a deceased person is still alive)

when needed, give clinical focus to support the family. The AAI has become a cornerstone with professionals who are working in adoption and kinship care, child protection, family law, and with refugees and immigration. Of course, having labels and a set of behaviours can help us to predict how others will react so that we can respond accordingly, but it can also be limiting for both the professional and the client. With only four categories relating to the whole human population, there will be times when clients feel unseen and unheard. Some criticisms of the AAI, and attachment theory more generally at that time, were that there was not enough nuance or thought for how attachment styles may change over the lifespan, as the research had been undertaken with parents and infants or young children. Now, we will introduce our final contributor to attachment theory in this brief story—Patricia McKinsey Crittenden.

Crittenden was a Master's student of John Bowlby and a PhD student of Mary Ainsworth, with her research focusing on the impact of child abuse and neglect. Prior to this, Crittenden had run a family centre for low-income and at-risk families, pioneering a video-feedback method of intervention to support positive change in the families. As with our previous attachment theorists, I would be interested to write about Crittenden's early life, but she has kept this private, preferring to focus on the work instead. Crittenden has had a global presence in attachment work and is still active in research and development in 2025. Crittenden's attachment standpoint is that human behaviours are organised to be self-protective, leaning on the idea that attachment behaviours are here to promote safety and comfort. She emphasised the importance of how our cognitive processes are strongly connected to our emotional processes, and this is what gives us the impetus to react in certain ways. I had the privilege of being supervised by Crittenden in 2021–2022, and her supervision changed the way I thought about my work, adding a real depth to my thinking. I had moved from being a rank-and-file music therapist to taking on a managerial role in a therapeutic practice, and Crittenden gave me the confidence to be bolder in my questioning and reflections so that I could support families and therapists in a more useful way. One of the questions on the SFF is, "How can you give the best of yourself to your client?", and this compassionate and authentic way really stuck with me. Even when not assessing families, I give this question to my own supervisees and students, as well as using it as a beacon for myself. It helps people (and me) to think about defences, drop those shoulders, and remember why we do this work. This is only part of what I have learned and carried through from Crittenden, and I always think it is important to acknowledge how our mentors have influenced us. So let's now move to how Crittenden was influenced by Bowlby, Ainsworth, and Main and to this final step in the creation of attachment theory.

In Crittenden's 2017 paper, Gifts from Mary Ainsworth and John Bowlby, not only do you get to hear about this golden thread of attachment theory development, but there is also this great sense of "gate-breaking"; that is, each researcher sharing their work in order to build the theory through others. Crittenden talks about how Bowlby spent hours with her, analysing clinical videos to support her in developing the CARE-Index for her Master's thesis. The CARE-Index is still in use today and is a 3-min video analysis of a parent playing with a child aimed at seeing how the family interacts in low-stress situations. Bowlby worked with Crittenden to detail the patterns of interactions, focusing on how responsive the parent was and if, in turn, the child was co-operative, compliant or passive. Bowlby's emphasis on understanding families through real-life observation was key in the development of the assessment tool. It was when Ainsworth returned from meeting Bowlby, sharing his first draft of "Loss: Sadness and Depression" with the students, that Crittenden found the language she needed to expand her own theories on attachment. In Bowlby's book, he stated that attachment was connected to how individuals process information and then "defensively exclude" parts of the information for self-protection. Crittenden began to expand the idea of how cognitive systems (predictable sequences in behaviours and reactions) worked alongside affective systems, that being how we process emotional signals to manage relationships to create a sense of safety. With the focus of Crittenden's work becoming "how do we use the information around us to keep safe?", she proposed that professionals needed to "change the danger, not the child", highlighting how perceived challenging behaviour in individuals reflected the environmental difficulties that they were tangibly facing.

To the experiences of working with Bowlby, Crittenden added Ainsworth's prominent methodological approach, ensuring that her own work was clearly evidenced. At this point, around 1982, Crittenden was creating parental assessment interviews which had the raised threat processes of the SSP alongside the added analysis of parental memory systems. Crittenden was bringing together the theories of the two "parents" of attachment theory, moving forward for a contemporary and individualised society. In Crittenden's 2017 paper, she reminds us that Ainsworth personally knew each of her research families from Uganda and Baltimore, insisting that researchers and professionals move beyond "tick boxes" and have the confidence to acknowledge individual needs in families through an attachment theory foundation. At a similar time, Crittenden was studying alongside Mary Main and her development of disorganised attachment. Whilst both agreed that Ainsworth's ABC attachment categories were not enough for individualised understanding, Crittenden disagreed that individuals presented as disorganised. Crittenden proposed that, in fact every behaviour was organised and being used as a strategy to keep the threat (whatever that may be) in a psychological place that would bring a sense of perceived safety. Attachment patterns became attachment strategies to Crittenden, using this to define the ways in which children may deploy a range of behaviours to maintain the availability of the protector. These theories all led to Crittenden creating the Dynamic Maturational Model—the DMM.

The DMM is a contemporary attachment model which expands traditional attachment theory. It describes interpersonal attachment relationships as flexible strategies that develop over the human lifespan. Like the model itself which deems attachment to develop over the lifespan, the DMM was created over many years—beginning in the 1980s with Crittenden's PhD, maturing in the 1990s with the design of several assessment tools, and finally coming of age in the 2000s, when the model was officially named in Crittenden's 2006 book, "The Dynamic-Maturational Model of Attachment". The DMM proposed that attachment behaviours are not a fixed set of personality traits but are actually self-protective and dynamic strategies employed by humans to protect themselves from danger, thereby ensuring the survival of ourselves and our progeny. Visually, the DMM differs from traditional attachment theory, too, with the complexity of human development shown in a flowing wheel rather than a table or simple labels (Fig. 2.2).

When I first started to learn about the DMM, it felt like a lot to take in—even the visuals are more complex. Each area of attachment theory is expanded and challenged so that they reach their full potential, creating complexity and depth to the original theoretical elements. Just as Bowlby and Ainsworth generously shared their knowledge with their students, so too will Crittenden and I explain the elements of the model as fully as possible, in an order as hierarchical as possible.

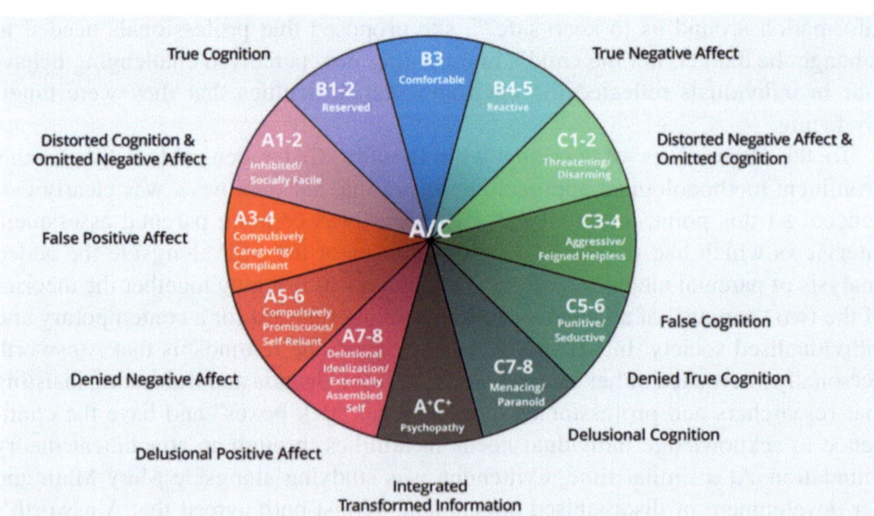

Fig. 2.2 The dynamic maturational model, copyright P. Crittenden

Attachment Categories

Whilst traditional attachment theory tells us that we have secure, anxious, ambivalent and disorganised attachment patterns, the DMM uses terminology relating to information processing to show us how we interact in attachment relationships. Depending on how we react in order to have our needs met, we may omit our feelings (affect) and prefer to rely on our thoughts (cognition) or vice versa. We may present as balanced in how we manage our feelings and thoughts, or we may chaotically move between the two. If we put this into attachment terminology:

- Type A—Cognitive Dominant (on the left side of the wheel). These individuals inhibit their own feelings from others and rely on using cognitive information to interact. These individuals are often "people pleasers", or "good children". In some instances, these people are sensible and rational. However, in more extreme instances, when the numbers on the wheel become higher, these people can omit (or split off) all of their so-called negative feelings and create a distorted sense of rationality in order to justify their masking. People with higher numbers of Type A will often have higher levels of psychosomatic conditions as they repress their feelings to avoid conflict with others.
- Type C—Affect Dominant (on the right side of the wheel). These individuals amplify their feelings (affect) in order to have their needs met. They will use many different strategies to gain attention, often in single interactions. This would be the child who asks for help and then rejects the adult offering the help. These individuals have distorted negative affect meaning that their more challenging feelings such as aggression will be present and they will be more likely to omit cognitive information. In the higher numbers of Type C, you will find people who gaslight others; being aggressive to someone and then saying that it didn't happen.
- Type B—Balanced (at the top of the wheel). The more secure attachment behaviours in the DMM are also presented on a spectrum. There is a true Type B, an individual who has had a very happy, content, trauma-free or distress-free life. Then there are B 1–2 and 4–5, who may have been through some challenges but are generally resilient, functioning well naturally or who have healed from their experiences and are now functioning well.
- Type A + C+ (at the bottom of the wheel). This is what would previously have been described as disorganised attachment. The individuals diagnosed as Type A + C+ will use chaotic behaviours to have their needs met and will present as very dysfunctional. These individuals will find it hard to function in society and may have enduring mental ill-health, have experienced extreme trauma or neglect, or be manipulative or malicious in a self-serving way.

Maturational Development

After reading the above descriptions of the DMM attachment strategies, it is important to note that we are not born with these levels of complexity. The DMM posits that attachment behaviours are not hard-wired in infancy but instead evolve as our levels of cognition do, through normal human development. As we physically, mentally and neurologically develop from infancy to older adulthood, we gain the capacity to process more and more complex contextual information, which enables us to deploy more complicated behaviours for self-protection. If we look at the diagram of the DMM above, we can see that the numbers associated with Type A and Type C move from 1 to 8. Each tranche of the wheel represents a different stage in development, with stages 1–4 appearing in childhood, and 5 upwards developing through adolescence to adulthood. Approximately 65% of the population remains as Type B with balanced and secure attachment strategies. If an individual experiences interpersonal difficulties and they do not have any support around them, they will move through the developmental attachment strategies as detailed in the DMM. Individuals do not always move through every tranche; they may stay at one stage, or, in the case of extreme trauma and neglect, move straight to the chaotic Type A + C+. In my clinical work with adoptive families, the category I have seen most of is A3–4 and C3–4. As the majority of children are adopted at the age of 3–5, this feels developmentally right for them to remain at the stage of attachment development. I have also often seen teenagers in A5–6 and some parents who remain at C5–6. With some therapeutic intervention, I have seen positive changes in individuals who present in these categories, and it really takes a network around the individuals to support this.

Attachment Strategies

By using the term strategy instead of pattern infers a sense of flexibility. If the reason we use attachment behaviours is to feel safe, then we have to deploy a range of behaviours in different contexts to feel this. Whilst in traditional attachment theory, an individual would be characterised as “secure” or “insecure” and presumed to use these behaviours in all contexts, the DMM states that actually humans use a range of conscious and unconscious strategies to interact with others and have their needs met. For instance, the way I relate to my husband, my children, my parents and my friends is very different—as it should be. In each role, I have a different need, as does the person I am interacting with. If I used the same attachment strategy in each context, this would be like using a hammer to fix all of my problems—it is not flexible or nuanced, and I may cause damage. If, however, I use a different tool that is suitable for each problem, then I am going to have much more success.

When we use a strategy, it is adaptive to that context. Context can be environmental (home or work), or it can be a person (parent or friend). This means that in that context—person or environment—we are using a strategy to interact with it so that we can feel safe and have our needs met. In a different context, with a different person or in a different place, this same adaptive strategy may not serve us and so becomes maladaptive; it is not effective to create safety, and the behaviours will feel out of place. Let's use an example. A child lives in a difficult home. Their parents may be suffering from enduring mental ill-health and alternate between being attentive and ignoring the child. The child has learned that to gain attention when they need it, they have to be loud and aggressive. When they do this, their parents turn their attention to their child, and the child gets what they need. The child, however, does not have another strategy to call on, so when they are in school, and the teacher or their peers are not listening, the child acts out aggressively. In this school context, where the child is expected to co-operate and take turns for attention, their adaptive home attachment strategies have become maladaptive.

Change the Danger, Not the Child

The DMM focuses on how humans adapt to danger, with our present attachment strategies being the physical manifestation of this. When we feel unsafe, we will act in ways to protect ourselves. This could be withdrawal, for example, or dissociation, aggressiveness, or oscillating between several behaviours. If individuals are using these strategies in a maladaptive way, as discussed above, instead of focusing on changing the behaviours, practitioners need to understand the feelings causing the behaviours. So, if we go back to our child acting out in school, we could put the child in isolation or punish their behaviour. If we try to understand the motivation and feelings causing the behaviours, however, then we can help the child to feel safe and to develop some other strategies to interact. If our child in school is not in any danger in that context and the professionals around them have offered layers of support, then we need to gain information on their other contexts to understand where the danger truly is. This leads us to another key Crittenden principle: by supporting parents to have more awareness of their child, professionals can support positive and enduring change in the family. As we have noted, maturation development happens when the individual is at the right age and stage. When professionals concentrate their efforts on the child solely, the child will only develop as much as cognitively possible, as determined by their age and their context. If we also include, or even focus, on the child's parents by developing their capacity to notice and respond to their child's attachment strategies, we can support the family to have new ways of being together and to address any intergenerational transmission of attachment behaviours.

The Professional as the Transitional Attachment Figure

Winnicott (1953), a British psychiatrist and family therapist (more information on Winnicott is in Part II of this book), proposed that to help children securely separate from their parents, they needed a support mechanism. This mechanism is often a physical object, such as a dummy, a teddy, or a blanket—you know, that special object we all remember having, and we see our children carry around with them (often never washed and seen in every early photo). The purpose of the object is to provide a physical representation of the parents or caregiver, which reminds the child that they are still loved and kept in mind, even though they cannot see their parents. The physical representation is used until the child internalises the feelings of "knowing" that their parents still love them and will come to collect them from school, and then, it will be discarded. The object is transitional as the child only uses it until they internalise the experiences they need to trust their parent or caregiver, after which they move on.

In Crittenden's DMM, the therapist, teacher, or social worker becomes the transitional object, and as they are usually a person of influence in the life of the individual, they become a transitional attachment figure. To be clear, the professional has the opportunity to positively affect the individual's dispositional representations for a preconceived attachment figure and therefore holds a transitional space in the interpersonal relationship between professional and individual where this can happen. Once the individual feels more settled and secure, they can discard (in the nicest possible way) the transitional attachment relationship, having internalised a new dispositional representation of attachment figures, ultimately breaking the cycle.

Assessment Tools

To help understand the experiences of families and individuals, the DMM has a unique suite of assessment tools, created by Crittenden and her collaborators, all aimed to highlight how behaviours are used for self-protection through information processing. The assessment tools cover the full human lifespan and are briefly detailed below.

Assessments for Birth to 5 Years Old

- Infant CARE-Index (0–15 months) assesses the dyadic interactions and parental sensitivity in a 3-min video recorded session.
- Toddler CARE-Index (15–72 months) uses the same structure as the Infant and includes a short play/frustration task.
- DMM-Strange Situation Procedure (SSP; 11–15 months) is a modified version of Ainsworth's SSP, which results in the use of DMM attachment classifications.

- Preschool Assessment of Attachment (PAA; 18 months–5 years) is a further adaptation of the SSP that aims to understand self-protective behaviours in the child.

Assessments for 6–13 Years Old—School Age

- School-Age Assessment of Attachment (SAA; 6–13 years) is an audio-recorded interview where children are asked to tell stories from picture cards, each one representing various levels of danger.

Assessments for Adolescence and Adulthood

- Transitional to Adulthood Attachment Interview (TAAI; 14–25 years) is a modified version of the Adult Attachment Interview (below).
- Adulthood Attachment Interview (AAI; 25+) is a structured interview, based on Main's work. The interview identifies how information is processed, the use of self-protective behaviours and also how memory systems are used.

A further DMM assessment is the Screening Family Formulation (SFF). This is a comprehensive interview which looks at every aspect of family life for each member of the family to understand the functional reasons for challenging or crisis behaviours. The SFF uses structured questions on Adverse Childhood Experiences (ACEs), an adapted version of Maslow's Hierarchy of Needs with attachment figures (below), as well as information on somatic conditions, reproductive and social systems. The SFF asks the professional leading the assessment to look for the discrepancies in the information provided by the family as this indicates where the omitted cognitive or affects are. The SFF provides useful recommendations on how the family can find ways to communicate and function differently in their daily lives (Fig. 2.3).

There are other emerging and useful assessment tools which can be used with the DDM or as a standalone. The Meaning of the Child Interview, developed by Dr. Ben Grey, uses a DMM theoretical framework. It is a semi-structured interview that focuses on parental sensitivity and how the parent understands the child and their behaviours. The tool is often used in child welfare cases and can help identify families who are at high risk of safeguarding issues. The Child Attachment and Play Assessment (CAPA) was developed by Dr. Steven Farnfield, a strong presence in the DMM community. The assessment is for children only and asks the child to tell narrative stories using dolls and toys. The result of the CAPA is an identified DMM attachment strategy, along with information on how the child can mentalise the experiences of others, how they relate to the interview and information on how trauma may be manifesting in the child's behaviours. This assessment tool is also used in child welfare and in adoption and kinship work. A final assessment tool which is useful is The Assessment of Parent–Child Interaction (APCI). The tool was developed by Prof. Stine Jacobsen, and I am heavily involved in this work, through leading training, research and delivery of the assessment. The APCI is unique in that it uses music as an analogy of parent–child interactions, providing information on parental capacity and potential attachment behaviours. The APCI consists of two

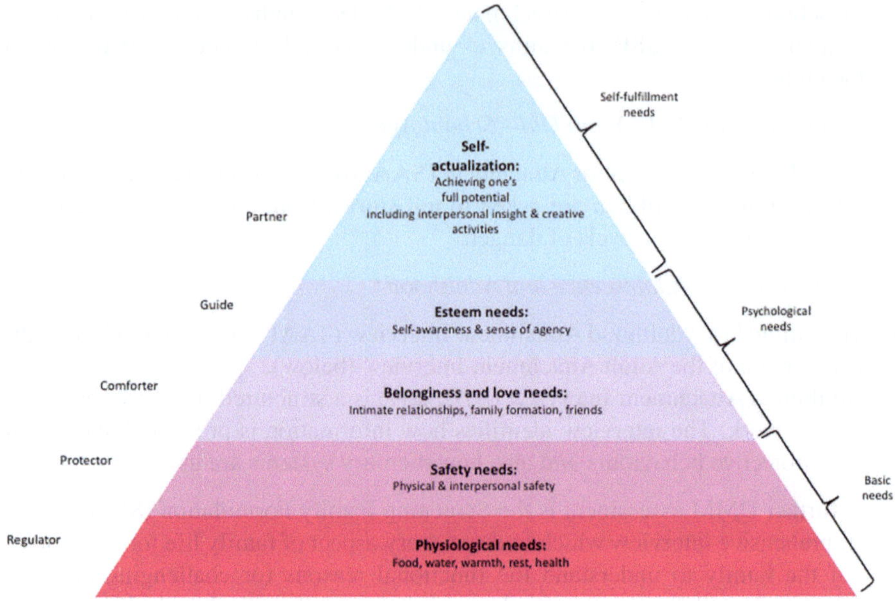

Fig. 2.3 Maslow's Hierarchy of Needs (1943), adapted by the DMM to include attachment needs. Copyright P. Crittenden

25-min recorded music sessions, with four dyadic activities. It has excellent test–rest validity and is used across the world. I often use the APCI alongside the SFF in my clinical work as the two assessment tools work well together in gathering a holistic picture of the family.

Information Processing

Throughout the descriptions of the DMM, we have talked about processing information, but what does this mean? In every interaction and situation we experience, we are receiving sensory, cognitive and emotional information into our brains and bodies. The DMM posits that we will process this information differently according to our attachment experiences. We could relate this to our Internal Working Model, as described by Bowlby, our stored behavioural template that helps us predict how a situation will unravel. As the DMM has moved away from preference for interpersonal stability to adaptation to perceived danger, the internal process of transforming the information has to reflect the need for protection. Dispositional representations (DRs) are an expanded version of IWM, which acknowledges the neurobiological importance of our reactions, along with the need for flexibility (as with our shift from patterns to strategies, model moves to representations). When our DRs are triggered, it means that information has been received and processed by the brain, and the brain has taken a shortcut based on a previous and similar event to react. The trigger—or the internal representation—*disposes* us to act in a certain way in order to keep safe. For example, if a child has learned that when they are sad, their tears are not acknowledged, their DR for sadness may be to not cry. So far, this sounds similar to an IWM, but the DMM recognises that to create that DR, the individual will have omitted or falsified cognitive or affective information in order to create a DR that helps them to feel safe. The child who smiles instead of crying when they are sad, therefore, has omitted their affect (sadness), overriding it with a distorted cognitive reaction, leading us to believe that they use Type A attachment strategies. When the child feels sad, they are disposed to react in an opposite way based on the representation they have stored internally.

A Strengths-Based Theory

When we think of the child described above, we may feel that not acknowledging their real feelings is a negative thing. Certainly, as a therapist myself, I would actively encourage my clients to own their feelings and say them aloud. With attachment theory, we are always thinking about the feelings underneath the behaviours. If we use the DMM to inform our thinking, then the behaviours and feelings move from being negative/insecure or positive/secure to being classified as "clear survival behaviours". The actions we take in every situation become adaptive to that context and are something we need to do in order to survive. By focusing on what the client did to survive, we focus on their strengths and resilience; we give them permission not to feel shame. This can contribute to a good therapeutic alliance and an increased sense of self for the individual.

The DMM is still being developed by researchers and professionals across the globe, and you can find out about those involved and the opportunities to learn about the DMM at the Family Institute website (see references).

We have come to the end of our attachment history journey for now. In this chapter, we have covered the progression of attachment theory through five decades and seen how Bowlby's wish for each generation of researchers adds to his foundations. Below is a timeline of the steps taken in this chapter, and we will now use this deeper understanding of information processing and transformation to think about how we construct our realities and societies.

Attachment theory development timeline		
1967	Ainsworth's SSP	Ugandan and Baltimore projects completed, leading to attachment classifications and maternal sensitivity
1973	Bowlby's IWM	Bowlby describes how humans internally store information to help predict behaviours in others
Late 1970s	Main's disorganised Attachment coined	Main observes behaviours in children uncategorised by the traditional three categories
1981	Crittenden's CARE index	Work with Bowlby to develop an observational tool to support parents and children
1985	Main's AAI	Main develops the AAI to understand those uncategorised behaviours and begins the work on the intergenerational transmission of attachment patterns
1992–1997	Crittenden develops lifespan attachment assessment tools	Crittenden develops several tools using qualitative and quantitative methods to understand the why underneath the behaviours
2006	The DMM is officially named	The DMM brings together all previous research with nuance and depth, acknowledging the complexity of human life
2008/2015	Crittenden's "raising parents" is published	"Raising parents" is a seminal text for all professionals working with families focusing on changing the danger and not the child

Chapter 3
Constructivism

The theories of constructivism and constructionism refer to the development of the human psyche and how we construct knowledge and experience, working in perfect harmony with IWM (Bowlby, 1973) and Dispositional Representations (DRs; Crittenden, 2015). The terms and theories of constructivism and constructionism are often used interchangeably, however there are key differences which are explored here. Constructivism explains how we build knowledge inside our heads, whilst constructionism argues that we build knowledge most effectively with something outside of our heads; something we can see, share, or critique. These are the simple answers, and we can keep these in mind whilst we read about the narrative of knowledge construction; constructivism and constructionism in action!

Jean Piaget was born in Switzerland in 1896. In the same year, Lev Vygotsky was born in Russia. In an unusual twist of fate, both men brought constructivism to social consciousness; however, their personal lives meant that their professional careers became very different. In our narrative here, I am going to begin with Piaget. The order will make sense once we reach Vygotsky.

Piaget was a precocious talent, and by the age of 11, he had written his first scientific observational article. His father, Arthur Piaget, was a professor of Medieval Literature, which could have been the motivation for Jean's theoretical and academic interest, although Piaget said that it was his mother who inspired his career. Rebecca-Suzanne experienced enduring mental health problems and was described as someone who would lose her sense of reality. Piaget's mother was put on trial during his childhood, accused of slander. She was a staunch Socialist and in opposition to the German politics of the time. According to Piaget's biographers (Quinn, 2019), he felt "deeply uncomfortable" with the feeling of abstraction and chaos, and sought to create sense in the "concrete" scientific observation of animals and then, later, humans. As observers ourselves, we can see that Piaget was possibly influenced by both parents in ways of which he was not fully aware. Interestingly, and like our previous theorists in this book, Piaget also underwent psychoanalysis and was a member of the Swiss Society of Psychoanalysis from 1920 to 1936. Early in

R. Swanick, *A Clinical Guide to Interpersonal Constructs and Attachment Theory*, https://doi.org/10.1007/978-3-032-23728-6_3

his career, Piaget would acknowledge the importance of mother–child relationships and observations, eventually, rejecting Freud's ideas of sexual desire being the driver for all human motivation. He would also go on to highlight his preference to focus on humanity as a whole rather than the individual, as in psychoanalysis.

In 1918, Piaget completed his PhD in Zoology. His interest in epistemology—the origins of knowledge—drove him in a different direction and, after studying with Carl Jung and Eugen Bleuler, he moved to Paris to work at the Alfred Binet Institute. Alfred Binet was a French Psychologist (b.1857—d.1911), whose name even now is synonymous with IQ testing. Binet and his colleague, Theodore Simon, developed the Binet–Simon test, which aims to assess the mental capacity of children through 30 practical and structured tasks. The test would score the results of the tasks and give the child a 'mental age', providing information for schools on the child's ability related to what they could do rather than their chronological age. The Binet–Simon test led to the creation of the IQ test—first William Stern (1912) divided the mental age by the chronological age to give an IQ score, then Lewis Terman (1916) multiplied that number by 100, giving us the Terman–Binet IQ test, which we use today. By the time Piaget began work at the Institute in 1919, he was working with Theodore Simon directly to determine if the tests were appropriate for children. In the administration of these tests, Piaget noticed "productive errors"—children were making the same mistakes each time, not due to their lack of capacity, but owing to their age and development and not having the skills *just yet*. He noticed that children had different logical reasoning than adults, and instead of focusing on the quantity of mistakes (as the Institute wanted), he was drawn to the quality of the mistakes. Piaget became interested in the "why" behind the mistakes. Using his psychoanalytic training, he created a more flexible interview, which he called the "clinical method", to converse and discuss with the children about their experiences and behaviours. He was interested in how children constructed their knowledge and how their active minds were influencing their experiences. That children were making mistakes related to their age highlighted to Piaget that knowledge was constructed developmentally, through assimilation and accommodation, rather than something innate. We know from our work with Bowlby earlier in the book that this was something that he struggled with too—the push to move the healthcare and psychological professions from the notion of the passive accumulation of knowledge to an understanding of experiential and developmental knowledge. By exploring children's experiences more freely in the interview, Piaget could observe the mental structures they were creating and living. This became the "process of coming to know", a core component of Piaget's constructivist theory.

Piaget's Constructivism

With his experiences and observations, Piaget created a theory that defined how children actively create their knowledge through experience. In Piaget's theory, humans store and organise the information they learn in "cognitive schemas"; the definition of a schema here is a "pattern of learning" (1964). These internal frames provide a structure for how we use knowledge to make sense of the world. Piaget believed that our schemes move from the simple—an infant reaching for something—to the abstract—an understanding of complex emotions in later life. *(A behavioural psychologist, B.F. Skinner, also used the term 'schema' and this refers to how our behaviours are shaped by rewards and consequences. We are not going to use this definition here but it is useful to know that there are other definitions out there.)* Piaget's schemas are created in three stages. Firstly, assimilation of knowledge, that is, by incorporating new information into existing schemas (adding a dog breed to the dog schema, for example). Secondly, accommodation of knowledge, which is where we change our existing schema to incorporate the new information or create a new one that is more fitting (realising that a cat is too different from a dog to be dog, and so a new schema, cat, is created). Finally, we need to find information equilibrium—sometimes new information causes "disequilibrium", and we need to find a way to accommodate the new information through further active learning. In my mind, schemas do not feel too distant to Dispositional Representations, with the difference being that DRs incorporate the emotional, behavioural and informational processing of information, whilst Piaget's schemas focus on how the information is stored cognitively.

As we noted earlier, Piaget had observed in his work with the Alfred-Binet Institution that children only learned what was developmentally appropriate for them, be that cognitively or chronologically. Subsequently, Piaget proposed that there were four main stages of development for children, which **were** related to their potential capacity at specific ages. The table below highlights the key characteristics of each stage (Table 3.1).

In summary, infants in stage 1 are concerned with sensing and doing, children in stage 2 are beginning to add symbols to language and experiences often without logic, children in stage 3 are beginning to use logic on real-life situations, and children in stage 4 become interested in thinking about knowledge assimilation and abstract possibilities.

Table 3.1 Piaget's four stages of cognitive development in constructivism, 1936/1952

Stage	Age (approx.)	Key goal/ achievement	Characteristics
Sensorimotor	Birth–2 years	Object permanence	Action-based: Learning through senses (touch, sight) and motor actions. No mental representation of objects yet.
Preoperational	2–7 years	Symbolic thought	Intuitive: Uses language and symbols (play-pretend). Characterised by egocentrism and difficulty with logical rules.
Concrete operational	7–11 years	Operational thought	Logical (concrete): Can perform mental operations on physical objects. Understands conservation, reversibility, and categorisation.
Formal operational	12+ years	Abstract reasoning	Scientific: Can think about hypothetical "what if" scenarios, use deductive logic, and grasp complex abstract concepts.

As Piaget's constructivism is a learning and applied theory, it might be helpful to think about how it is used in real life. A parent may engage in "peek-a-boo" with their child in the sensorimotor stage to help them develop object permanence, for example. To develop symbolic thinking, the caregiver might encourage some imaginative play, such as making a spaceship from a box. As the child grows, the caregiver might ask more open-ended questions or respond to the child's question with another question—"why do you think that happens?". In the classroom, free play is frequently used, and Maths may be puzzles and models rather than learned formulas. There will be opportunities for "flipped learning" where the students become the explorers and experts, sharing the knowledge they have gained with the rest of the class and the teacher. By creating this open space for active learning, the child begins to discover for themselves and develops a deep sense of curiosity for the world.

Naturally, there are some critiques of this form of constructivism. The methodology has been questioned many times—Piaget used a small, Western, middle-class sample (often the case in psychological research) to complete quite complex tasks. Furthermore, he used qualitative interviews to collect data, leaving the results open to subjectivity. This could lead to a lack of attention being paid to the impact of social factors on childhood development and the risk of confirmational bias from the researchers as they potentially analyse data based on their own understanding and experiences. As we saw in the development of attachment theory, it was important to note the influence of a child's whole life—family, home, school, socio-economic—to fully understand their development. We also saw that by adding quantitative elements to research, patterns of development were more easily defined and recognised. Of course, Piaget was working much before these academic findings, but perhaps it would be interesting to run those initial tests again to see if there is validity and rigour.

With this unanswered question from Piaget's constructivism on the impact of social factors on the child's development, we can move to our next contributor to the theory—Lev Vygotsky. Even though Vygotsky was born in the same year as Piaget, he grew up in Tsarist Russia, rather than a socialist-learning Switzerland, which meant that Vygotsky faced many career challenges. His family was middle-class and Jewish, with his parents being described as supportive. In fact, they would go on to inspire one of his most notable theories, but we will come back to that shortly. Vygotsky's father was a successful banker and philanthropist, founding a public library. His mother was a trained teacher, which was unusual for a woman at that time. As we saw with Piaget, these early learning influences and environments perhaps paved the way for Vygotsky to become the theoretician that he was—especially when we consider Vygotsky's slant on constructivism. Vygotsky was home-schooled until he was 15 and was also described as precociously intelligent, as with Piaget. Due to being Jewish and the socio-political environment in Russia, Vygotsky found it difficult to gain a place at university. He eventually won a place at Moscow University in 1913 by taking part in a ballot system, which was nicknamed the "Jewish Lottery", to study medicine. Vygotsky changed his mind part-way through, and by 1917, he had graduated with a degree in Law, whilst he had also simultaneously been studying for an Arts and Humanities degree at a private university. He returned to his home town to teach literature and psychology, and it wasn't until 1924 that Vygotsky found wider recognition. In the Second All-Russian Psychoneurological Conference of the same year, held in Petrograd, Vygotsky delivered three key papers: "The Methodology and Reflexology of Psychological Research", "How Psychology should be Taught Now", and "Results of a Questionnaire on the Moods of Students of the Graduating Classes of the Gomel Schools in 1923". Only the first paper that still exists today, and this paper gave him national recognition for his call to review new scientific ways to understand human consciousness.

For the following decade, Vygotsky worked in the Psychological Institute in Moscow, bringing new ways of working with physical and learning disabilities, producing many articles and books. In 1934, Vygotsky contracted tuberculosis and sadly died. He was only 37 years old. Vygotsky left much of his work unfinished, and with the growing changes in politics in Russia, his work became "politically suspect" and banned under the new Stalinist regime. Vygotsky's writing and research were only rediscovered after the post-Stalin "Thaw", and it wasn't until 1978 that his seminal book "Mind in Society" was published in English. *I am a big advocate for Vygotsky's work and use his theories frequently, so I often wonder what would have happened if his work had remained in prominent academic circles during this time.* The book publication led to a "Vygotsky Boom" in education. We will now look at the key elements of his work, and I hope you can begin to connect this to attachment theory.

Learning as a Social Construct

Vygotsky proposed that learning only happens in social contexts and developed Piaget's original theory into what we now term Social Constructivism. Whereas Piaget thought that learning happens within the individual and then is transferred as a social skill, Vygotsky proposed that learning experiences have to happen twice—once on a social level (between two people) and then on an individual develop (to fully internalise the learning). He used the term Interpsychological to describe how humans learn through social relationships and collaborative dialogue, and Intrapsychological to describe the process of humans internalising and transforming learning for their own unique cognitive knowledge. Piaget proposed that the development of speech is a transitional stage which moves from a voice created in the individual towards speech being used socially. Vygotsky proposed that speech develops as a result of social interactions, which then moves towards the individual knowing their "voice" or personality. This example describes the individual-centric view of constructivism versus the social-centric view of constructionism.

The Zone of Proximal Development

The Zone of Proximal Development (ZPD) is a psychic space where an individual can learn with the guidance of another individual. It is the space in potential for an individual: they could do the task up to a certain point, but then they would need help. The ZPD is encased in the inner circle, which is where the learner can do tasks independently, and the outer circle, those tasks which are too difficult even with help (see Fig. 3.1).

If we put this theory into practical terms, a child may be able to complete a 12-piece jigsaw independently and with ease. This means that they are working in their inner circle of development. A parent or educator may offer the child a 36-piece jigsaw. As this is a sizable step-up for the child, the adult will support the child to complete the jigsaw, offering techniques and guidance. This may be repeated multiple times until the child remembers. The child must also feel safe with their adult so that they can concentrate on the task at hand. This stage is defined as the child working in their ZPD in an interpsychological way. Once the child remembers their learning, that is that they have intrapsychologically learned a process, they will return to the inner circle state where they can work on the jigsaw alone, even at the higher level of complexity. If, on the other hand, the child had begun the 36-piece jigsaw without adult help and without the problem-solving techniques required for a complex jigsaw, they would have been working in their outer circle, where tasks are too difficult for their skill or developmental stage. A child who remains in the outer circle, without adult guidance moving them towards their ZPD, may become bored, frustrated, or experience learned helplessness, which will affect future attempts in their learning.

Fig. 3.1 Diagram of the inner circle, ZPD, and outer circle according to Vygotsky's theory

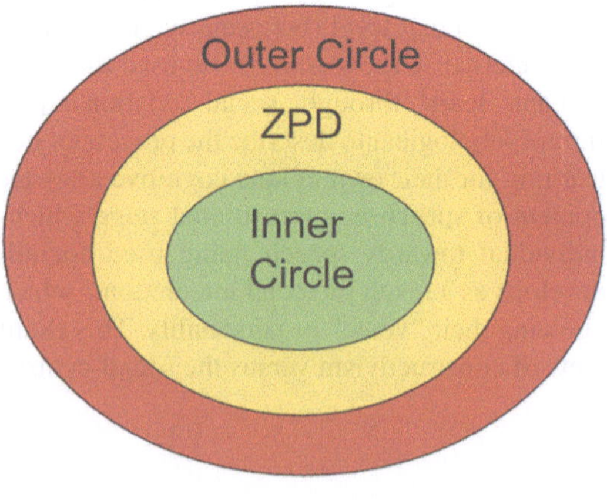

The More Knowledgeable Other

The More Knowledgeable Other (MKO), in simple terms, is the name for the person who helps the learner when they are in their ZPD. The MKO does not need to be someone older, a teacher or even an adult; it can be someone who knows about the topic or experience and is willing to support another with this. The MKO can be a peer, a fellow classmate who has already completed the maths problem, for example. It could be your child helping you to set up your mobile phone. It could be a therapist who is supporting you with your problem, or it could be a parent helping their little one to learn. A positive MKO will be someone who models ways to be, offers supportive questions, helps to break down tasks into chunks, or provides feedback on the completion of tasks. These will be undertaken consciously in some MKOs, like teachers and therapists, but often unconsciously, as in a friend or a parent. The ultimate aim of the MKO is to help the learner to internalise the social learning, moving from outer circle, to ZPD to inner circle, or from intrapsychological learning to interpsychological.

Scaffolding and Fading

The term "scaffolding" was not something used by Vygotsky, but it was added by Wood et al. (1976) when his work was published in the 1970s. It is a useful concept to think about, so I have added it here to help inform Vygotsky's theory to its fullest. Scaffolding is the name for the temporary support provided by the MKO when the individual is in their ZPD and learning a new task. The term is a metaphor and brings to mind a solid structure around an object, which we can translate into the helpful support the MKO offers through their interactions. Once the learner has mastered the task, the scaffolding is gently removed by the MKO, and this is known as "fading". The scaffolding provided is not meant to be permanent, and it is a reflection of Vygotsky's idea that the MKO first does the task, then the MKO and learner do the task together, and finally the learner does the task independently; "I do, we do, you do". If the scaffolding is used for too long, then the learner may become overly dependent, and if the scaffolding is not right, then the learner may become frustrated. It is integral that the MKO watch for nonverbal and interpersonal signs that they and the learner are feeling safe in the ZPD.

Language and Play

Vygotsky viewed language and play as "primary psychological tools" in human learning and development. Vygotsky observed that children initially use speech as a social tool and then, at around age 3, they begin "private speech". This is when children speak aloud to themselves during play, for example, or whilst problem-solving. Piaget saw private speech as an egocentric and sometimes "immature" process, whilst Vygotsky viewed this as a self-regulatory tool and a way to creatively solve challenges. By age 7, Vygotsky noted that speech moves from a social tool to an intellectual tool, with a child's inner speech becoming more complex and limited to their inner voice. For Vygotsky, thought did not exist independently; it was shaped by the child's culture and the language that was happening around them.

Vygotsky found that play was integral to a child's development as it neatly placed them in their ZPD, enabling them to practice skills they had yet to develop in their daily lives. Vygotsky stated, *"In play, a child always behaves beyond his average age, above his daily behavior; in play, it is as though he were a head taller than himself"* (1978, *pg. 102)*. He noted that play helped children to develop abstract thought (the box becoming a spaceship). Role-play, he observed, helped the child to practice social interactions (being a parent in the game or taking turns) and executive functioning (organising the game, being self-regulated whilst in character). In this way, language and play become intertwined in Vygotsky's theory, with language providing external scripts for play before being internalised as social constructs and higher cognitive functioning.

As we are building theoretical knowledge on how humans store (or possibly do) information, whether that be cognitive or interpersonal, I will now describe the differences between constructivism and constructionism, with some definitions of constructionism. I find it is important for us to know as much as possible to decide which theories 'talk to us'. My own positionality statement for learning theories is that I am committed to Vygotsky, and we will go back to this in connection to attachment theory later. You might find something that resonates in other theories, so please explore your own thoughts and fall down the rabbit hole if it suits you.

Whilst constructivism wonders about the internal processes of learning and knowledge acquisition, constructionism posits that we learn by externalising what we do into a creative process. Seymour Papert (1928–2016) was a computer scientist, mathematician and teacher based in the USA, although he was born in South Africa during apartheid. Papert worked with Piaget in Switzerland from 1958 to 1963 with the aim of understanding how children build mathematical knowledge. Piaget described Papert as the "most brilliant protege", and they both believed that children should be active learners in their educational journey. Papert diverged from Piaget in his disregard of children's learning in formal stages. Papert also believed that children were capable of understanding and processing very complex information, ultimately leading to his belief that computers should and could form the cornerstone of school education. Papert noted that children learned most effectively when they created an external and "real" version of their knowledge—this could be a model, a computer programme, or an image. These "objects to think with" (Papert, 1980) become "external mirrors" for the mind. The externalised objects can direct representations or be reconstructed in order to process new ideas. If a child makes a sandcastle, they may follow some instructions given by an adult or copy an image.

In this instance, they can see how the object is constructed, how the shapes fit together, why a square base works best, etc. If the child chooses to reconstruct the sandcastle, they can explore if the square base is indeed best, which shapes fit together and which do not, etc. This links to another element of Papert's constructionism—making mistakes, or de-bugging, is essential to learning. Papert believed that the process of making errors is where humans can do their deepest thinking and reflection, and used the term "metacognition" as a description. A further term used by Papert was "bricolage". Generally, bricolage means to use what you have available to create something. Papert's definition, however, has more energy as it means to "tinker" or "play" with something in order to see how it can be manipulated. Constructionism rejects traditional teacher-learner situations, instead insisting that the teacher becomes a facilitator providing materials for the learner to explore through construction, for the furtherance of the learner's own goals, rather than a curriculum. Papert actively encouraged education settings to focus on the "art of learning" rather than pedagogy.

In theory, Papert's theory offers a lot of flexibility and freedom to students and educators. However, in my experience, students need to build knowledge and have a foundational understanding of core subjects in order to have the skills to explore more advanced situations. If we link this to Vygotsky's zones of learning, it could be that the student in Papert's context is perpetually in the outer circle (Fig. 3.1), and without input from A. N. Other, will never experience the peace of being comfortable in the inner circle. We can link this feeling to attachment theory; with so much freedom and without the necessary scaffolding, the student may become dysregulated and frustrated. The openness of constructionism may become counterproductive for learning. Additionally, thinking of teachers, it would be very difficult to assess learning, to be an expert in every subject and to ensure students learn the necessary skills they need for life and work with the freedoms Papert describes as the cornerstone of education. It would be difficult for students to fully understand complex mathematical structures, for example, without input from another person. A further criticism of constructionism is around the impact of socio-economic backgrounds of children having an impact on their learning—children from supportive, or wealthy and educated families may have an advantage in their foundational knowledge when compared to children from challenging backgrounds. As we have found with attachment theory and constructivism, there seems to be an individual stance (early psychoanalysis and Piaget, for example) and a systemic view (Bowlby and Vygotsky), and the same is true of constructionism. So, let us now turn our attention to Berger and Luckmann's work on social constructionism.

Peter Berger (1929–2017) was born in Vienna and emigrated to the USA before World War II. He initially wanted to be a Lutheran Minister but diverted his career to sociology, famously saying that he was an "accidental sociologist". As a result of his career path, Berger's attention was firmly on religion and humanistic philosophies, and he eventually founded the Institute of Culture, Religion and World Affairs at Boston University. Thomas Luckmann (1927–2016—I am interested that they were born in the same years and worked together, as did Piaget and Vygotsky—was born in Yugoslavia (what is now Slovenia) and went on to study in Vienna and

Innsbruck, before moving to the USA in 1950. The philosophers met when they both became influenced by the ideas of Alfred Schutz. An interesting character in his own right, for most of his life, Schutz was a high-level city banker during the day and a philosopher and writer in his spare time. Schutz is considered the founder of "phenomenological sociology", which in simple terms is the idea that humans live in a "common" world with shared understanding by co-creating social structures which provide rules, order and limitations on how to behave and interact with each other. Berger and Luckmann were inspired by these ideas and wrote their groundbreaking text, "The Social Construction of Reality" in 1966, with the aim of grounding Schutz's ideas in everyday life experiences.

"The Social Construction of Reality" is a dense text, but an enjoyable read, and it still has many relevancies in today's world. The book is a "treatise" on how humans construct knowledge as a society. The foundational idea of the work is that humans collectively construct a shared reality based on their own internalised rules and expectations, ultimately believing that this reality is fact. Berger and Luckmann proposed a three-step "core process": humans internalise the meanings of objects and social rules, then externalise them by acting in accordance with those rules and meanings, leading to the meanings and rules being objectified (solidified or made true) through human interactions over time.

To explain in a different way, if I have an apple in front of me and I tell you that it is an orange, you can choose to dispute it or believe it. If thousands of people say that the apple is an orange, then, theoretically, it will be an orange as we all believe it to be so. In this example, I have externalised my internal thought and then objectified the meaning of the object through my interactions. When we reflect on our society as we experience it, we can see how this process is completely present and relevant. We can apply this to the role of gender in society—in the West, we live in a patriarchal society where male figures mainly hold the power and female figures still have fewer rights to work, in healthcare and often hold a vulnerable position in relationships. This can be extended to sexuality, with LGBTQ+ people experiencing less tolerance than cis-het people. If we think about race and culture, people from different backgrounds are more often than white people to experience hate crimes and discrimination. In cultures outside of the West, other constructs have different weightings.

There are communities in China, India and Africa that are matriarchal and male figures have less systemic power. White people may hold the power in the West, but that is definitely not true in Arab states, many African communities or in China. These are small examples of the huge problems that society has created and that we are perpetuating through this core process of internalisation, externalisation and objectifying terminology and rules. We can link this to attachment theory: if we are what we repeatedly do (see DRs), then we will be what we always have been, according to social constructionism, too. If we want to see positive change, then we need a circuit breaker to gradually adapt to what is internalised, externalised and objectified as a society. Perhaps this has to start on an individual level with our self-responsibility, and then I think we have a case for the importance of all of the theories described so far as comfortably co-existing and working together. We will come back to this collective theory idea in our coming chapters, so let us now return to the social construction of reality.

Berger and Luckmann believed that language holds a high level of importance when humans are constructing their societies. Language is a symbol or a "constitutive" which actively builds our view of the world through labels, categories and framing. The concept of parenting or being a parent is defined by our societal expectations of the role, and how we frame the language associated with concepts provides more expectations. The terms "single parent" and "co-parenting" have different connotations for society, with single parent often being seen as a negative situation, whilst co-parenting is considered the most positive way to parent. Neither terms nor expectations take into consideration the systemic issues around the single or co-parenter, but instead assume something built on the societal constructs of previous experiences or expectations. This leads to two other aspects of the theory, that of mutual reconfirmation and institutionalisation. This is how we confirm the constructs we have created through everyday interactions and conversation. When we speak to each other, and we use the same labels, categories and framing, we are confirming our view of reality and are unconsciously agreeing that this view is still the truth. This is present in the labels we use and the roles we create for people. The aim of mutual reconfirmation is to affirm what we know so that the knowledge doesn't change, and the aim of institutionalisation is to provide societal order and predictability (*this person is a policewoman and therefore I can trust them, for example*).

A criticism of Berger and Luckmann's theories at the time was that the book underplayed the importance of power and inequality in relation to language, although we can also see in their theory that power is ever-present in social constructionism, as it will always be the group with the loudest voice that influences how society behaves. The reason we have minority groups in our communities is that the group with the most power has constructed our society this way. The language that powerful groups use provides "norms" for how we perceive others—how would we know that a criminal is bad and a doctor is good—and it legitimises certain terminology to gate-keep knowledge away from the general public so that power remains. Obvious examples of the use of language and power are in politics and healthcare. Politicians use labels and framing, especially to drive the message of their political party—think "War on Drugs" and "Take Back Control". The healthcare profession will often use language in patient diagnosis and with other professionals that maintains the hierarchical structure of paternalism. In these ways, Berger and Luckmann's theory cannot be criticised for underplaying power and language in society, as their book states their own truth on what they believe the facts of how societies are built.

This chapter has provided us with a rich exploration of constructivism, social constructivism, and social constructionism, situating them within broader debates about how humans develop knowledge, meaning, and psychological organisation. We have begun to explore the links between these learning theories and attachment theory, internal working models (Bowlby, 1969), and dispositional representations

(Crittenden, 2015), developing an argument for an integrated understanding of cognitive, relational, and socio-cultural development.

We have explored Piaget's constructivism, thinking about Piaget's emphasis on the individual learner, noting both its strengths—particularly the recognition of children as active meaning-makers—and its limitations, including methodological concerns, cultural bias, and insufficient attention to social and relational contexts. These limitations served as a bridge to Vygotsky's social constructivism, which re-centres learning as fundamentally social, relational, and culturally mediated. Vygotsky's core contributions—the distinction between interpsychological and intrapsychological learning, the zone of proximal development (ZPD), the more knowledgeable other (MKO), and the processes of scaffolding and fading—are closely aligned with attachment theory. Learning first occurs between people and only later within the individual, contingent on safety, trust, and relational attunement, and with language and play being central to this development.

We then moved to constructionism, beginning with Papert's educational constructionism. While acknowledging Papert's emphasis on creativity, externalisation, and learning through making, it was also noted that with insufficient scaffolding of learners, and viewed through an attachment lens, there are potential risks for dysregulation, inequity, and exclusion.

Finally, the chapter examined Berger and Luckmann's social constructionism, focusing on how shared realities are produced through processes of internalisation, externalisation, and objectification. Language provided a central mechanism through which power, norms, and institutions are maintained and legitimised. We discussed power and inequality, finding that social constructionism could be seen to implicitly reveal how dominant groups shape "reality" through language and institutional authority.

As we move into our next chapter on personal and then family constructs, we will use these foundational theories to move through to contemporary construct philosophy. Below is a timeline of our construct journey so far.

Construct philosophy development timeline		
1919	Piaget's productive errors	Piaget begins work at the Alfred Binet Institute to test IQ and notices the importance of errors.
1929	Vygotsky is noticed	Attendance at the Second All-Russian Conference brings Vygotsky to a national audience.
1936	Piaget's develops his theory	Piaget writes about his stages of development, still in use today.
1966	Berger and Luckmann publish "The Social Construction of Reality"	This seminal text brought social constructionism to a global audience.
1978	Vygotsky is published in English	After decades in exile, Vygotsky's work is finally brought to the West and starts "Vygotsky fever" in educational professionals
1980	Papert publishes "Mindstorm"	Papert's first text on constructionism and how externalising the internal could be helpful

Chapter 4
Personal Constructs

In the previous chapter, we looked at four strands of construct philosophy from 1919 to the 1990s. There are other theories on how humans construct knowledge, and we are going to explore two of those other strands here. Initially, this may feel counterproductive as we are going back quite a few decades. This, though, is really a sideways step that will help us to get to our final destination in Chap. 5.

Our timeline from this chapter ended in 1980, and it is to 1955 that we return. "The Psychology of Personal Constructs" was written by George Kelly in 1955. Kelly (1905–1967) had an erratic start to life. His Presbyterian minister father and school teacher mother decided to move the family from Kansas to Colorado in 1907, in a wagon, in a bid to claim free land. The American government had created a bill called the Homestead Act of 1862, which entitled settlers to claim ownership of any land they had lived and worked on for 5 years. The government asked only $18 from the settlers to buy the land, and this enabled many families—poor, immigrants, formerly enslaved—to escape poverty and gain control over where and how they lived. At the time, the American South still had many oppressive rules in place, and the Federal Government was actively promoting settlements in the West of America to encourage a large farming community rather than slave-based plantations. The Kelly family stayed in Colorado for 4 years and eventually returned to Kansas when their American Dream was destroyed by the lack of water. Kelly had been home-schooled throughout this time, and this continued until he was 13, when he went to boarding school. Despite his unconventional start to life, Kelly had a healthy experience in higher education, completing an undergraduate degree in Physics and Mathematics in 1927, an MA in Educational Sociology in 1928, a Bachelor of Education in Scotland, UK, in 1930, and then his PhD in Psychology back in America in 1931.

When Kelly returned to America, the country was in the depths of the Great Depression. This economic crisis began in 1929 with a catastrophic stock market crash and resulted in the loss of businesses and industry over many years. In 1933, at its peak, unemployment was around 25%, with some states seeing up to 80% of

R. Swanick, *A Clinical Guide to Interpersonal Constructs and Attachment Theory*, https://doi.org/10.1007/978-3-032-23728-6_4

people without jobs. This obviously affected society intensely, with hundreds of thousands without work, unable to pay rent for homes or healthcare, or buy food. This also coincided with a decade-long drought, and farmers could not grow crops to supply food. Psychologically, this marked a change in attitude to the American Dream, something that the Kelly's may have already experienced. Suicide rates heightened whilst marriage and birth rates dropped. For America, it would take almost a generation to see recovery, and it wasn't until 1941, when the government increased spending for World War II, that the population started to see improvements.

It was during this time of the Great Depression and the Dust Bowl drought that Kelly initiated a scheme he called "Traveling Clinics", whilst teaching at Fort Hays Kansas State College. The aim of the project was to provide medical and psychological support to children, families and teachers working in the rural communities that had suffered most in the economic downturn. The project became so successful that it was eventually funded by the local government and could be seen as the pilot scheme for modern healthcare systems across the West. In this service provision, Kelly noticed several patterns in how the patients responded and expressed their needs. He found that psychoanalysis, which we know was popular during the 1930s, was irrelevant for a farmer or family who had lost everything due to natural disasters, or a decision made well outside of their circle of concern. The attendees of the clinic wanted a way to make sense of their troubles, and Kelly and the team became adept at "framing the chaos" with logical reasons. Kelly even experimented with this idea, sometimes providing a frame that made societal sense but was a platitude. This too brought comfort to the patients. This realisation formed the foundation of Kelly's key theory in the realm of construct philosophy.

"Constructivist Alternativism" (1955) is the idea that whilst there may be one true reality happening in human consciousness, we each experience it differently based on our personal experiences. *We construct alternative versions of reality based on our experiences of relationships and the environment around us throughout our lives.* In Kelly's theory, there is flexibility, as the version of reality we have construed will change depending on our most current understanding of the issue at that time. A simple example could be that perhaps we like an actor in a film as they portrayed a good person with similar characteristics to ourselves. We might then watch one of their other films where they play someone we don't like, and this changed view of them becomes our new opinion of them. We can choose to go with this opinion, or revert back to our first opinion, or even find another way of feeling. We might have made up our minds about the film actor based on our mood at that time, whilst our friend who watched the film with us may have a completely different opinion based on their mood, or their own moral code about right and wrong. Both opinions of the film actor are "right" as they are held by the individuals based on their life experiences. We can then choose to agree to disagree or listen to each other and bring a shared construct of the film actor into being. Kelly believed that individuals behave like "scientists", continuously testing and retesting hypotheses of how others will react and how situations will play out. If we continue our example with the film actor, as we have watched one film where the actor is likeable and one where they are not, we could watch a further film to confirm or deny our constructs of the actor. Of course, when we think about construct philosophy, these "experiments" often happen internally, although they do occasionally happen externally, too. Kelly proposed that when testing new constructs, individuals notice their existing systems (feelings and thoughts about something), internally anticipate how the situation will go, experience the situation and notice the behaviours within it, then either create a new construct based on new behaviours and reactions or confirm their existing system. With our film actor, we have constructed that they can be a likeable person, we watch the third film with a prediction of them being likeable, the actor behaves terribly in the third film, and we create a new construct that the actor is unlikeable overall. The figure below (Fig. 4.1) shows a comparison of Kelly's process with a scientific methodology.

As we explore our reality in this scientific way, Kelly highlighted that we can have autonomy in how we build our narrative for life. The goal of the human journey is not to find an absolute truth but instead to construct our own truthful reality that helps us navigate our experiences. In constructive alternativism and to stick with the film analogy, we are the main character of our lives, with the choice to create new plots or continue with the ones we know. Kelly called this "freedom from biography", stating, "No one needs to paint himself into a corner; no one needs to

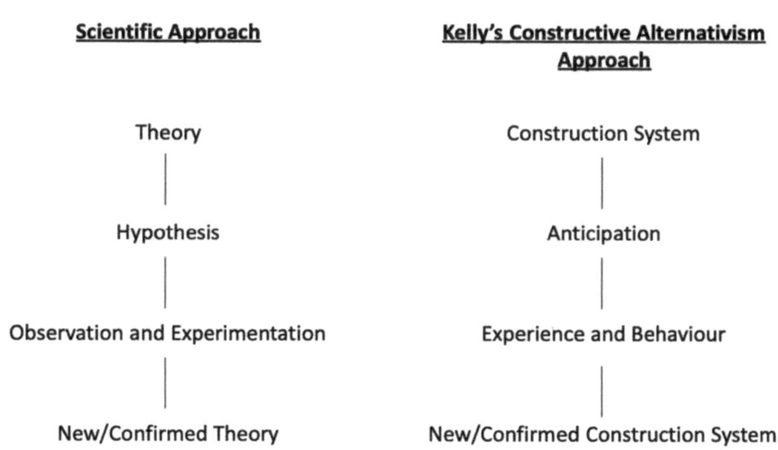

Fig. 4.1 Kelly's constructive alternativism approach, where clients become "scientists" in the therapeutic process (Boeree, 2006)

be completely hemmed in by circumstances; no one needs to be the victim of his biography" (1955, pg. 15). As a person becomes aware that they need to change their constructs of a situation, they will take on the process of reconstruing which is a reconstructive process. The person may do this in a therapeutic or learning relationship, exploring new ways of being to allow for personal change. If the person finds a new way to manage a situation, they will adopt the alternative construct as it will now have predictive efficiency, meaning that it enables the person to predict the outcome of the situation in a better way.

Now, let's take a minute to think about this. The aim of this book is to think about attachment theory and construct philosophy, and there has been a small elephant in the room—and that is the question "why?". Why are we thinking about this? Why is this important and relevant? We got a little bit closer to this question and answer in linking Vygotsky with attachment theory, and I think with Kelly, we have made the Venn diagram. In both constructivist alternativism and attachment theory, the individual internalises their experiences in an individual way, and this causes anticipation in constructivist alternativism or disposes us to react in attachment theory in certain ways in certain situations. As each person's reality is made up of these individually viewed experiences, there are many alternate realities happening every minute of every day. In both constructivist alternativism and attachment theory, we can either follow the path we have been given through intergenerational transmission—through interpersonal relationships or socially constructed norms—or we can, with some external input, create new constructs or strategies for attachment.

We can add another element here to the Venn diagram by adding Vygotsky. Kelly proposed that the reconstruing of information happens usually in a therapeutic or learning relationship, or, as Vygotsky stated, with the more knowledgeable other. Let's add attachment theory to the diagram and say the parent or transitional attachment figure, and we have built a complex foundation for understanding how humans learn, develop and care for each other (Fig. 4.2).

To think about this even more deeply, attachment theory is a theory (of course), and the definition of a theory is something that offers an explanation for a particular phenomenon in a specific area. Constructivist alternativism and social constructionism are philosophies; philosophy being something that offers a much broader view of a foundational way of thinking about knowledge and values, for instance. With this all in mind, does attachment theory explain the presenting behaviours for the feelings created in construct philosophy, and are they inextricably linked? I am committing to this and saying, yes, yes, they are, and I will continue to explain this over our next chapters. For now, we need to return to Kelly as there is so much more to say.

In 1955, Kelly published a book titled "The Psychology of Personal Constructs", which gave a clinical shape to his philosophy of constructive alternativism. As briefly stated above, a philosophy is a foundational idea of how we think about

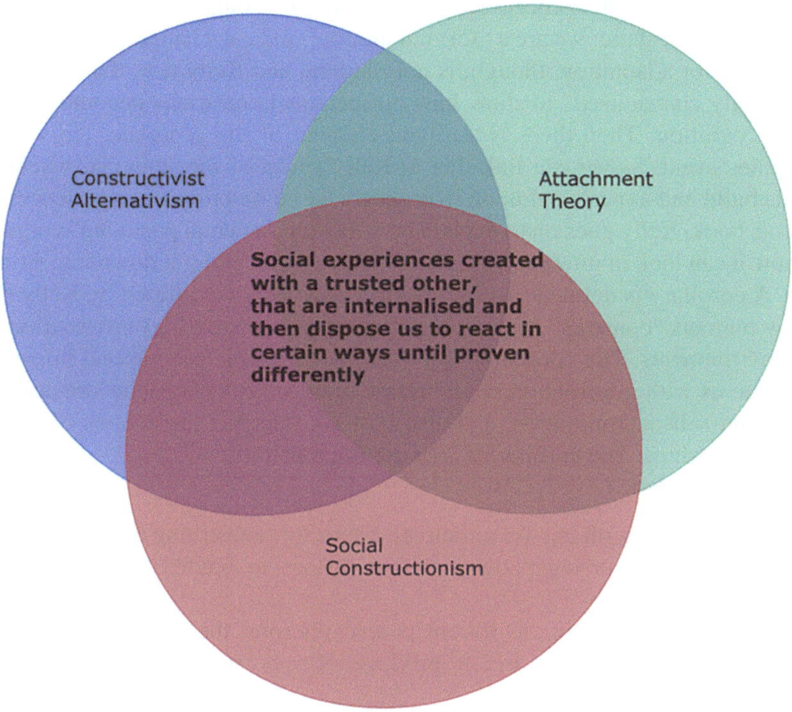

Fig. 4.2 Venn diagram of constructive alternativism, attachment theory, and social constructionism. Author's own

values, whilst a theory is more specific, relating to a specific area of work. Whilst Kelly had given us information on how we construct knowledge as individuals, he also told us how we could use it. In his book, Kelly rejected behaviourism and the notion that humans are reward-activated; he rejected the idea that humans are driven by unconscious motivations as in psychoanalysis, and firmed his argument that humans are active agents (scientists) who create internal cognitive templates relevant to themselves only; that is, they construct a personal narrative for their lives. Our personal constructs provide a way for us to predict the future as we test and refine the best way to interact with others and our environments. Kelly proposed that we have two areas of constructs. Core constructs are those that are integral to our values and experiences and are much more resistant to change. Peripheral constructs are more pliable and are easily modified if needed. These ideas led Kelly to create a fundamental postulate, a kind of motto to guide us in how we think about personal constructs. The postulate states that "a person's processes are psychologically channelised by the ways in which he anticipates events". If we break this down, Kelly uses the term "person's processes" to describe our thoughts, feelings and behaviours. We are not static; we are a "form in motion" and can change/adapt constantly. This change or adaptation, though, is not random, and Kelly uses the phrase "psychologically channelised" to show how our personal constructs become our structure of cognition. Then there is the final element of the postulate, "in which he anticipates events"—we can link this to Kelly's idea of the scientist, where individuals build and experiment upon hypotheses based on previous experiences.

In his book, Kelly goes on to explain how this fundamental postulate is organised and how it can look in interpersonal relationships by breaking it down into 11 corollaries. A corollary is defined as a proposition, and each one offered by Kelly shows us how humans "construe" (that is, the process of constructing) information from their environments. The corollaries show us how we structure internal information to provide us with information on the future, how we can choose information with agency and self-determination, and also how we interpret the actions of others to build relationships. The corollaries are simplified below.

The 11 Corollaries

1. Construction Corollary: We anticipate events by "construing their replications". We look for recurring patterns in our history to predict how future events will unfold.
2. Individuality Corollary: Different people interpret the same event in unique ways. Our constructs are a product of our personal experiences and perspectives.
3. Organization Corollary: We organise our constructs into a hierarchical system of ordinal relationships. This allows us to move efficiently from one piece of information to another.
4. Dichotomy Corollary: A construct system is composed of a finite number of bipolar constructs (e.g. "kind vs. cruel"). You cannot understand one end of a construct without its opposite.
5. Choice Corollary: We choose the side of a dichotomous construct that we believe provides the best opportunity for extending or defining our system—balancing security with growth.
6. Range Corollary: Each construct has a limited "range of convenience". For instance, "friendly vs. unfriendly" is useful for social interactions but not for describing weather.
7. Experience Corollary: Our construct systems change as we successively construe the replications of events. We learn by adjusting our "hypotheses" when predictions fail.
8. Modulation Corollary: The variation in our construction system is limited by the permeability of our constructs. Permeable constructs more easily admit new ideas.
9. Fragmentation Corollary: A person can use a variety of construction subsystems that are "inferentially incompatible" with each other. This explains how an individual can behave inconsistently in different roles.

10. Commonality Corollary: To the extent that two people use similar constructions of experience, their psychological processes are similar. Sharing a culture often means sharing a similar set of constructs.
11. Sociality Corollary: To effectively interact with another person, we must understand how they construe their world. This "getting inside their head" is essential for playing a role in a social process.

Kelly designed the Repertory Grid to help therapists understand their client's internal corollary systems. The grid is a structured interview which asks the interviewee to think about a specific area of their life (relationships, work). The interviewee is then encouraged to make connections based on the dichotomous corollary with the aim of understanding what moral and ethical constructs they hold internally. For example, the interviewee may want to understand more about their relationships. They would choose three people, and the interviewer will ask, "in what important way are two of these people alike and one different?". One could be content, whilst the other two are frustrated. This is repeated multiple times until the interviewer and interviewee discover no new dichotomies. The interviewer can then help link the answers together and highlight the constructs that the interviewee holds dear.

By understanding our internal processes through the framework of the corollaries and the repertory grid, Kelly illuminated that we could see where information was hidden, thus revealing the unthinkable feelings and thoughts the person was experiencing. If we go back to the analogy of our film actor, what is the underlying message in the script that they are not telling the audience? What are they choosing to show us (the choice corollary), what constructs in them can be modulated, what is shared in commonality, etc.? I find the dichotomous corollary most helpful in therapeutic situations as it shows that humans are multidimensional and not just "good" or "bad". In fact, the dichotomous corollary suggests that we can't actually have feelings without their opposition. So, for bad to exist, for example, there needs to be good (an opposite), as otherwise everything is bad because that is the only thing we know. We don't know what bad is unless we have first experienced good. Another way to think about this would be if you were rich and you lived only with rich people, then not only would you not know what poor is (the opposite), you would also not have a word for rich, as it would be assumed that everyone you knew lived that way. Opposites—or dichotomies—provide a boundary for us to think about something different, and these experiences will change constantly throughout our lives based on where we are contextually. Constructivist alternativism is the belief that all of our current interpretations of the world around us are subject to revision. We will come back to this proposition and associated ideas in our next chapter, and it also provides a good link to our final subject in this chapter—Family Constructs.

Harry Procter (2017, 2022; Ugazio & Dixon, 2013) first coined the terms "family constructs" and "relational construct psychology" in reaction to the theories created by Piaget (1952), Vygotsky (1978), and Kelly (1955). Procter noticed that the individualistic concepts of Piaget and Kelly did not fully acknowledge the experience of being in a family and felt that constructivism was "ripe" for being explored within the context of constructionism. Procter completed his PhD in Personal Construct Philosophy in 1978 at the University of Bristol. He is a renowned clinical psychologist and is still very active today, writing books and articles, providing supervision and mentoring and as a Visiting Professor at the University of Hertfordshire. I have had some interesting discussions with Harry in recent times about philosophical terminology, and he always brings so much energy and thought to our conversations. Similarly to the attachment theory researchers, Procter is a "gate-breaker", actively encouraging new thinkers into the construct philosophy community and being very giving of his time. Anecdotally, it does feel unusual for researchers to be so open with their knowledge; in the therapeutic profession, much of the work and knowledge is monetised; those creating interventions, for example, fiercely defend the information that is shared. So when I hear of researchers who are secure in their work and willing to open up the discussion for new ideas and innovations or to guide others, I feel heartened, as the "gate keeping/breaking" is definitely one of my own dichotomous constructs, and I really enjoy working with all generations of researchers.

Procter's research began with personal constructivism and then moved to systemic constructivism, a term coined by Procter which focuses on how individuals construct experiences relationally within families. In his clinical work, Procter noted that families build their version of reality together through co-construction. This version of constructivism details how the family reacts as individuals based on their personal experiences to build a social network of constructs available only to the family. The family is a meaning-making system which aims to maintain the patterns required to keep the family safe. There is no single problem in the family when we apply systemic constructivism as a philosophy, instead the problems are a result of the entire system repeating and maintaining their patterns. I have used the group of "family" here, but we can apply the philosophy to all groups, such as workplace organisations, educational groups and friendship groups. If we go back to definitions of philosophy and theory, systemic constructivism provides us with the "how"; underlying information to describe how groups construct knowledge. So, then, we need a subject-specific theory to provide the "what"; what are the specific ideas the family holds? To this, Procter proposed the theory of Family Constructs.

Family constructs recognises that individuals construct information based on their personal experiences of being within a family social network. They are the internal maps that families use to predict and maintain family life, often becoming shared templates for how families view the world. Dichotomous constructs become imperative within the family as most family values are created to make the family feel safe—a kind of "them vs. us" type feeling. When we think of our own families, we can notice the values that we feel are important. Statements like "we are hard working", or "we are cultured", or "we are sporty" may be said out loud or held subconsciously to affirm the identity of the family as something unique when compared with others. If a music-loving family is invited to a football match by a sport-loving family, they may say, "no, thank you; that is not our thing", both confirming their constructs and creating an opposition construct in which to measure their identity. In Kelly's (1955) work, he would call the opposite constructs poles (I visualise this like the North and South Poles on the globe). The poles can be something in our consciousness that we are aware of (emergent), or they can be hidden and unconscious (submerged). With our music-loving family, their emergent pole is that of enjoying music, perhaps having a favourite collective musician. Their submerged pole could be that of sports and activity; perhaps they have some misconceptions about sportspeople, or they were not chosen for games when at school. Of course, I am simplifying here for the purposes of the example, but hopefully you can see how we can create opportunities to affirm who we are and what we believe in by hiding or rejecting a construct in opposition to that.

The family creates these dichotomous, social and identity constructs by continuously repeating their patterns. Procter proposed that in this context our constructs are created in a circular nature: Person A speaks/acts, Person B returns speaks/reacts, Person A speaks/reacts, etc.; each person changes the previous statement of intent, thereby creating and expanding the construct. The family construct becomes a system created by continuous interactions within the group and reflection within the individual. Ugazio and Dixon (2013) described this as creating a family plot, a narrative that the family constructs their lives around, with each family member taking a role in the plot. If we return to dichotomous constructs in the family plot, the narrative could be that everyone in the family enjoys music (and other interests are submerged) or each member of the family has their own interests with some shared, and there is more balance in the family (more emergent poles). More importantly, if we take out the surface-level cultural identity analogy, each member of the family will hold a role which upholds the narrative of the group—and this is where difficulties can arise when thinking therapeutically and in an attachment-focused way. For example, if the mother is very powerful, then everyone else in the family may have to be submissive (the opposite) in order for the family to function in its usual pattern. If the son becomes more powerful, the pattern is disrupted; the family are unsure how to react, as this is different, and an emotional crisis can occur for the family. To use attachment theory language, the function of the mother being powerful whilst everyone else is submissive is adaptive in that context, as it keeps the family safe. When the son tries something new, the original pattern becomes maladaptive as the dynamic and needs have changed. The point here is that the family constantly chooses to affirm or reject their adaptive patterns in order to affirm or reject their family constructs.

To think about this fully, Procter developed the "bow-tie" diagram (Fig. 4.3; Procter, 2017), which emphasises how constructs are reinforced through relational interactions in the family.

In the bow-tie diagram, we can see the family set out in four corners and the potential patterns of interaction shown by arrows. The mother in this situation is feeling distant from her son, and the father is taking extra special care of the son's needs. The son's attention seems to be consumed by the father, and therefore, the mother is left out, no matter what she does to join in. To dive deeper into this, the more the father does for the son, the son will become more reliant upon him and perhaps resentful of his mother, who he feels does nothing for him. The mother will

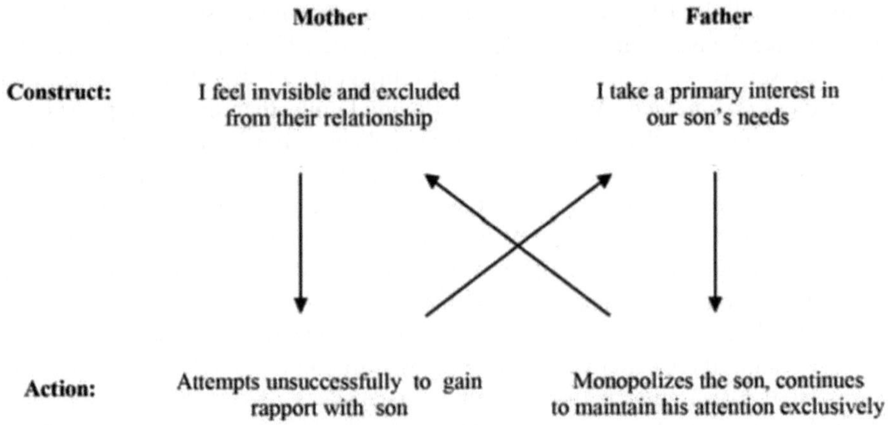

Fig. 4.3 Bow-Tie diagram of the reinforcement of constructs through relational interactions (Procter, 2017, pg. 74)

probably keep trying a little while and then give up, reinforcing the opinion that the father gives all and that she does nothing for her son. Resentment will then build between father and mother—father will feel all-powerful and right, whilst mother will feel angry at father taking her place and may become withdrawn from the family. Unless there is a circuit breaker in the family constructs, these patterns of interaction will continue to take place, affirming the dispositional representations of Mother, Father and Son for each family member.

To understand the constructs of the family, we can use the bow-tie diagram to notate our observations and findings, and we can use the techniques and "laddering" (Hinkle, 1965) and "pyramiding" (Landfield, 1971) to gain the information.

Laddering

We can use this technique when our client has a very specific problem and their emotional reaction is high. In laddering, we are asking "why is this important?" so that we can sense the value or construct underneath the reaction. To use the technique, you take a statement and then ask why, looking for responses that hold feelings or behaviours in opposition. At each stage, there will be a dichotomous construct which the individual is using to measure the values or performance of the other, whether that be spouse, family member or friend. In the example below (Table 4.1), the parents are arguing over the tidiness of the kitchen. One parent is "laddered" first to understand how they are constructing their reactions.

In Procter's systemic constructivism, we would then repeat the exercise with the other parent and ascertain their personal constructs. In this example, perhaps the other parent feels that messy = relaxed = not my parents = freedom. Once we have

Table 4.1 Example of an imagined laddering conversation in therapy. Author's own

Question	Therapist	Client response	The new construct
Start	"Which is better to be, tidy or messy?"	"Tidy, obviously".	Tidy vs. messy
Step 1 (up)	"Why is it important to be tidy?"	"Because it means you are in control of your life rather than chaotic".	In control vs. chaotic
Step 2 (Up)	"And why is being 'in control' better than 'chaotic'?"	"If you're in control, you're reliable. If you're chaotic, you're failing".	Reliable vs. failing
Step 3 (Core)	"And why is being 'reliable' the most important thing here?"	"Because being reliable means you are worthy of love. If you're a failure, you'll be abandoned".	Worthy vs. abandoned

Table 4.2 An imagined conversation in therapy for pyramiding. Author's own

Level	Therapist question	Response (Person A: "Reliability")	Response (Person B: "Freedom")
The Core	"You both want to feel safe. How do we define that?"	"I need to know the house is a *secure base*".	"I need to know I'm not in a *prison*".
Step 1 (Down)	"What specific behaviors make you feel 'secure' vs 'imprisoned'?"	"Knowing what to expect when I walk in the door".	"Being able to decide my own schedule without a lecture".
Step 2 (Down)	"What is an *example* of an 'expected' vs 'flexible' kitchen?"	"The counters are clear of food scraps before bed".	"Leaving the pans to soak until the morning if I'm tired".
Step 3 (The Deal)	"What's a middle-ground behavior?"	"I can handle soaking pans if the counters are wiped".	"I can wipe the counters if I don't have to scrub the pans yet".

the two personal constructs from each parent, we can work together to make a shared construct so that instead of having two core values that don't seem to relate to each other, the parents can acknowledge the worries around worthiness and abandonment, whilst also having their needs for freedom met.

Pyramiding

This technique has a similar method and outcome, except it works best with abstract feelings and thoughts (rather than concrete examples). Instead of working upwards as in laddering, by pyramiding, we are working down through the feelings until we get to the specific need. In the example below (Table 4.2), the therapist asks for more information on the parents' feelings. Once the feelings have been named and explored, the parents can look at the specific actions and behaviours they can each address to support positive interactions. The aim of pyramiding, as with laddering, is to create a shared construct with a flexible approach that supports the needs of both individuals.

In this chapter, we have traced the development of constructivist thought from Kelly's personal construct psychology to Procter's systemic and relational approach, situating these ideas alongside attachment theory and social constructionism. Across these perspectives, a consistent theme emerges: human experience is not passively received but actively interpreted, negotiated, and reshaped within relational contexts. From the individual "scientist" testing hypotheses about the world, to families co-constructing shared narratives and identities, meaning is continually produced through interaction. Techniques such as the repertory grid, laddering, and pyramiding demonstrate how these internal and relational processes can be made visible and open to change, offering powerful tools for therapeutic and developmental work. If systemic constructivism is a process by which individuals make sense of their experiences, we can come back to attachment theory through Durant's (1926) interpretation of Aristotle's quote, "we are what we repeatedly do" (pg. 87). In both constructionism and attachment theory, the individual's patterns of interaction become reactive to their environment. When viewed through the lens of attachment theory, these constructs take on additional significance, revealing how early relational patterns shape anticipation, emotional regulation, and responses to others. Together, these frameworks provide a coherent foundation for understanding how people learn to relate, adapt, and transform across the lifespan. As we move into the next chapter, this integrated perspective will allow us to deepen our exploration of how attachment and constructivist processes intersect in practice, and how they may be harnessed to support resilience, growth, and meaningful change. We complete the chapter with an updated developmental timeline for construct philosophy, now including Kelly and Procter

Construct a philosophy development timeline		
1919	Piaget's productive errors	Piaget begins work at the Alfred Binet Institute to test IQ and notices the importance of errors.
1929	Vygotsky is noticed	Attendance at the Second All-Russian Conference brings Vygotsky to a national audience.
1936	Piaget's develops his theory	Piaget writes about his 'Stages of Development', still in use today.
1955	*Kelly publishers "The Psychology of Personal Constructs"*	*Seminal text on constructivist alternativism and personal constructs*
1966	Berger and Luckmann publish "The Social Construction of Reality"	This seminal text brought social constructionism to a global audience.
1978	Vygotsky is published in English	After decades in exile, Vygotsky's work is finally brought to the West and starts "Vygotsky fever" in educational professionals
1978	*Procter publishes PhD*	*Procter's PhD thesis on systemic constructivism and family constructs*
1980	Papert publishes "Mindstorm"	Papert's first text on constructionism and how externalising the internal could be helpful
2013+	*Procter and Ugazio publish on family constructs*	*Brought family constructs to contemporary and wide audiences. Convergence of many elements of constructivism for the benefit of the family practitioner and clients.*

Chapter 5
Bringing It All Together: An Introduction to ICAT

Over the past century, psychology has witnessed the emergence of multiple theoretical traditions seeking to explain how human beings develop, regulate emotion, construct meaning, and relate to others. Among the most influential of these are attachment theory, constructivist and constructionist epistemologies, and personal and systemic construct psychology. Although often treated as distinct intellectual movements, these traditions share a common concern with the relational, interpretive, and developmental processes through which individuals come to understand themselves and their worlds. This chapter argues that these bodies of work are not merely compatible but deeply interconnected, forming a coherent framework for understanding human development, adaptation, and change.

Attachment theory, originating in the work of Bowlby (Bowlby et al., 1953) and later developed by Ainsworth (Ainsworth & Bell, 1970), Main (Main & Weston, 1981), and subsequent researchers, established the foundational insight that early relational experiences shape patterns of emotional regulation, expectation, and interpersonal behaviour. Bowlby's synthesis of psychoanalytic thought, ethology, and systems theory reframed attachment as an evolutionary adaptation designed to promote survival through proximity-seeking and caregiving relationships. Ainsworth's strange situation procedure empirically operationalised these ideas, identifying secure, avoidant, ambivalent, and later disorganised attachment patterns as observable relational strategies. These classifications demonstrated that children's behaviour reflects not fixed traits, but adaptive responses to relational environments.

Subsequent developments in attachment research extended this framework beyond infancy into adulthood and across generations. Main's work on the adult attachment interview revealed how early relational experiences are encoded in narrative and reflective processes, highlighting the role of coherence, mentalisation, and representational systems. The concept of internal working models further emphasised that attachment is not merely behavioural, but cognitive–affective, involving anticipatory schemas that guide perception, interpretation, and action.

R. Swanick, *A Clinical Guide to Interpersonal Constructs and Attachment Theory*, https://doi.org/10.1007/978-3-032-23728-6_5

Later models, including Crittenden's Dynamic-Maturational Model (2006), expanded attachment theory to account for contextual risk, information processing, and self-protective strategies, situating attachment patterns within broader ecological and developmental systems.

Running parallel to these developments, constructivist and constructionist traditions were articulating complementary accounts of how human beings come to know and interpret their experiences. From Piaget's genetic epistemology (1964) and Vygotsky's sociocultural theory (1978) to Berger and Luckmann's sociology of knowledge (1966), these perspectives challenged realist assumptions about cognition and emphasised that knowledge is actively constructed through interaction, language, and culture. Learning and development were increasingly understood as relational achievements rather than individual accumulations of information. Vygotsky's notion of the more knowledgeable other, for example, foregrounded the interpersonal mediation of cognitive growth, resonating strongly with attachment theory's emphasis on caregiving relationships as developmental contexts.

These philosophical traditions also raised critical questions about power, inequality, and social positioning, highlighting how meaning-making is shaped by historical, cultural, and institutional forces. Knowledge is not neutral but embedded in social practices and value systems. This insight complicates purely individualistic accounts of development and invites greater attention to the relational and political dimensions of psychological functioning.

George Kelly's theory of personal constructs (1955) provides a pivotal bridge between attachment theory and constructivist philosophy. Developed in the context of the social and economic upheavals of the Great Depression, Kelly's work emerged from practical engagement with communities facing profound insecurity and loss. His concept of constructive alternativism proposed that individuals actively generate interpretive frameworks through which they anticipate and organise experience. Rather than being driven by unconscious impulses or conditioned responses, people function as "scientists", continually testing hypotheses about themselves, others, and the world.

Kelly's emphasis on anticipatory systems closely parallels attachment theory's internal working models. Both frameworks conceptualise human behaviour as guided by internally organised expectations shaped through relational experience. His distinction between core and peripheral constructs mirrors the relative stability and flexibility of attachment strategies, while his notion of reconstruing resonates with therapeutic and developmental processes of change. The fundamental postulate—that psychological processes are channelled by anticipations—captures the dynamic interplay between past experience, present interpretation, and future-oriented action.

Kelly's elaboration of this postulate through his 11 corollaries further articulates how individuals organise meaning, manage contradiction, negotiate identity, and participate in social systems. Constructs are inherently bipolar, culturally situated, and relationally enacted. The repertory grid and related techniques demonstrate how these internal systems can be made visible and explored, offering practical methods for understanding emotional and relational difficulties.

While Kelly's work foregrounded individual meaning-making, later developments extended construct psychology into explicitly relational and systemic domains. Procter's systemic constructivism (2017) and Ugazio and Dixon's family construct psychology (2013) addressed the limitations of individualistic models by situating personal constructs within ongoing interactional patterns. From this perspective, families and groups function as meaning-making systems that co-construct shared narratives, identities, and expectations. These shared constructs regulate behaviour, maintain stability, and define boundaries between "us" and "them".

Family constructs operate through circular processes of communication and reinforcement, producing what Ugazio terms "family plots" within which members adopt complementary roles. These narratives are not merely descriptive but normative, shaping what is perceived as acceptable, dangerous, or desirable. The bow tie model illustrates how relational patterns stabilise particular positions and emotional responses, often constraining individual agency while preserving systemic coherence. In attachment terms, such patterns represent adaptive strategies for maintaining relational security, even when they become developmentally limiting.

Techniques such as laddering and pyramiding operationalise these ideas in therapeutic contexts, enabling practitioners to trace surface conflicts to underlying value systems and attachment-related fears. These methods reveal how dichotomous constructs—such as control versus chaos, worthiness versus abandonment, or autonomy versus dependence—are embedded in relational histories and emotionally charged meanings. Through collaborative exploration, families and individuals can develop more flexible, integrated constructs that support both security and growth.

Viewed together, attachment theory, constructivist epistemology, and personal and systemic construct psychology converge on a relational model of human development. Across these traditions, individuals are understood as embedded in networks of meaning that are historically situated, emotionally structured, and continually negotiated. Early attachment relationships provide the initial templates for interpreting experience, regulating affect, and anticipating others' responses. These templates are elaborated through cognitive and cultural processes, becoming personal and shared constructs that guide behaviour across contexts and over time.

Importantly, this integrated perspective challenges deterministic interpretations of early experience. While attachment patterns and core constructs exhibit relative stability, all three traditions emphasise the possibility of change through relational engagement. Vygotskian scaffolding, Kelly's reconstruing, and attachment-informed reflective functioning all describe processes through which individuals can revise entrenched patterns within supportive relationships. Development is thus neither linear nor fixed, but iterative and relational.

At the theoretical level, this synthesis also invites reconsideration of the relationship between theory and philosophy. Attachment theory offers domain-specific explanations of relational behaviour, while constructivism and constructionism provide broader epistemological frameworks for understanding knowledge and value. Personal and family construct psychology occupies an intermediate position, translating philosophical assumptions into clinical and developmental practice. Together, these perspectives suggest that attachment phenomena may be understood as the lived expressions of deeper constructivist processes operating within relational systems.

Therefore, attachment, personal meaning-making, and social construction are best understood as interdependent dimensions of human functioning. Emotional regulation, identity formation, learning, and interpersonal adaptation emerge through the ongoing interaction of biological predispositions, relational histories, and interpretive practices. By integrating these traditions, we gain a more comprehensive account of how people learn to relate, how difficulties become organised, and how change becomes possible. The model, therefore, becomes Interpersonal Constructs and Attachment Theory (ICAT), and the diagram below explains how the two theories work together (Fig. 5.1).

In every interpersonal interaction, we are called to make a choice on how to react to and integrate information. We either predict or anticipate, depending on whether we are following attachment or constructivist theory, how a situation will go based on past events or new information. The outcome of our predictions or anticipations will affirm or challenge our dispositional representations. We could even go as far as saying "dispositional constructs", depending on how we view the model, as it is our internal representation or our internal construct that disposes our behaviours. We will then react in a way that helps us have our needs met, and the attachment strategy loop is completed. Each ongoing interaction contains this same cycle, with our brains choosing the most efficient (and well-used) route most of the time. To change the cycle, we need an More Knowledgeable Other (MKO) to put an obstacle in the way, causing our brains to find another way to get our needs met. We cannot learn or change without understanding our interpersonal viewpoints—how does it feel when we are with others, how do they feel when they are with us, what do we need and give to others, and how do we give and get these needs met… This is the ultimate dichotomous construct—are we really ourselves if there is not one there to reflect us? As professionals, we have chances and a responsibility to provide opportunities for positive change in all of our client relationships. I remember when I first started teaching, my mentor told me that every interaction is a chance for a positive interaction, and I carry this with me even now, decades later. We can be the change for someone (Fig. 5.2).

In the chapters that follow, this integrated framework will be developed further through detailed analysis of clinical practice, developmental trajectories, and intervention strategies. There will be further information on therapeutic and support techniques which we can all use to make our client-focused interactions meaningful. By situating attachment processes within broader constructivist and systemic contexts, the aim is to provide a theoretically coherent and practically useful foundation for understanding resilience, vulnerability, and transformation across the lifespan.

We will end this chapter with a synthesised timeline that includes attachment, construct and personal construct theorists.

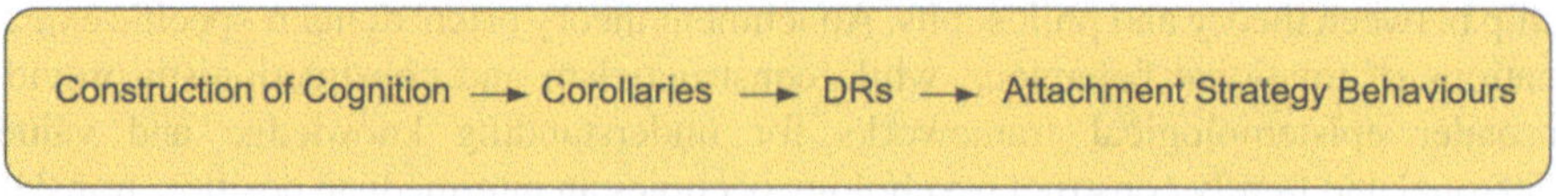

Fig. 5.1 Linear diagram of constructionism (Piaget, 1952; Vygotsky, 1978), corollaries (Kelly, 1955) to attachment theory (Crittenden, 2015). Author's own

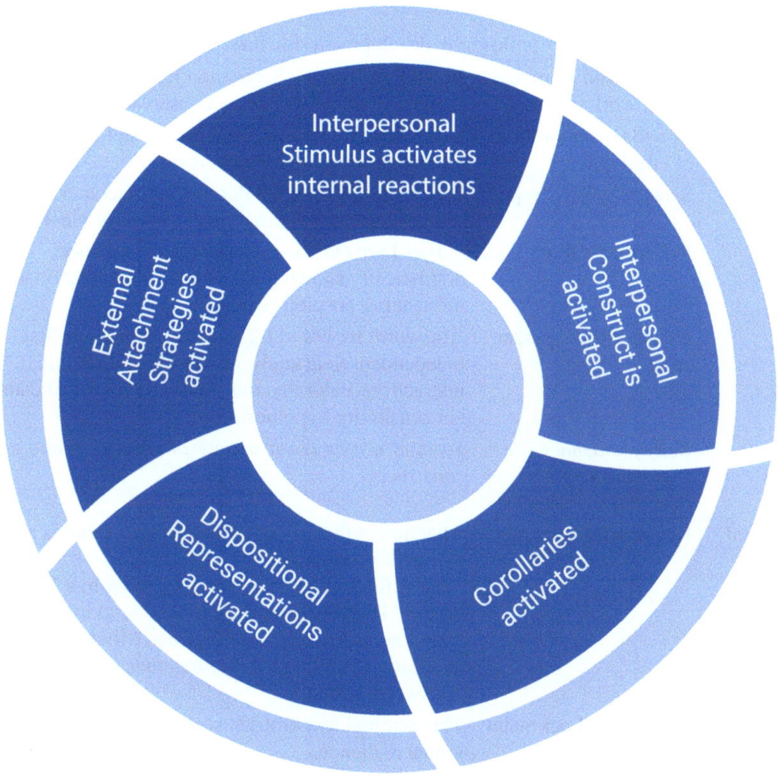

Fig. 5.2 Cycle of interpersonal relationships and subsequent constructs and behaviour processes. Author's own

Attachment theory & construct philosophy development timeline		
Early 1900s	Freud's Cupboard Love	Dominant psychoanalytic view: attachment is a learned, secondary drive based on food provision and pleasure.
1919	Piaget's Productive Errors	Piaget begins work at the Alfred Binet Institute to test IQ and notices the importance of errors.
1920s–1940s	Klein's Object Relations	Influential psychoanalytic theory focusing on the infant's internal world of fantasies about "objects"
1929	Vygotsky is noticed	Attendance at the Second All-Russian Conference brings Vygotsky to a national audience.
1930s	Bowlby begins at the Tavistock Blatz's Security Theory	John Bowlby observes the link between maternal loss and later delinquency. William Blatz develops "security theory", influencing Ainsworth's focus on secure dependence as a base for exploration
1936	Piaget's develops his theory	Piaget writes about his "Stages of Development", still in use today.
1944	Bowlby's "Forty-four Juvenile Thieves Study"	Links early, prolonged maternal separation to the development of an "affectionless character"

(continued)

(continued)

Attachment theory & construct philosophy development timeline		
1948	Bowlby and Robertson begin work together	Bowlby sets up the Separation Research Unit and hires James Robertson to conduct observational studies.
1950s	Bowlby's exploration of ethology	Using key theories and concepts from Lorenz to provide a foundation for attachment theory
1951	Bowlby's WHO report	Puts forth the maternal deprivation hypothesis, arguing that continuous maternal care is vital for mental health.
1952	Robertson's film	*A Two-Year-Old Goes to Hospital* is released, dramatically showing the distress of separation and influencing hospital policies.
1954	Ainsworth's Ugandan study	Ainsworth moves to Uganda and begins her first independent field study, observing mother-infant interactions naturally and gathering empirical data for her sensitivity hypothesis.
1955	*Kelly publishers The Psychology of Personal Constructs*	*Seminal text on constructivist alternativism and personal constructs*
1956–1960	Key articles released	Attachment theory begins to take shape and is addressed to a wider audience. "The Effects of Mother-Child Separation: a Follow-up Study, "The Nature of the Child's Tie to his Mother, "Separation Anxiety and Grief and Mourning in Infancy and Early Childhood" bring together Bowlby and Ainsworth's theories
1966	Berger and Luckmann publish The Social Construction of Reality	This seminal text brought social constructionism to a global audience.
1967	Ainsworth's SSP	Ugandan and Baltimore projects completed, leading to attachment classifications and maternal sensitivity
1973	Bowlby's IWM	Bowlby describes how humans internally store information to help predict behaviours in others
Late 1970s	Main's Disorganised Attachment coined	Main observes behaviours in children uncategorised by the traditional three categories
1978	Vygotsky is published in English	After decades in exile, Vygotsky's work is finally brought to the West and starts "Vygotsky fever" in educational professionals
1978	*Procter publishes PhD*	*Procter's PhD thesis on systemic constructivism and family constructs*
1980	Papert publishes "Mindstorm"	Papert's first text on constructionism and how externalising the internal is helpful
1981	Crittenden's CARE Index	Work with Bowlby to develop an observational tool to support parents and children
1985	Main's AAI	Main develops the AAI to understand those uncategorised behaviours and begins the work on the intergenerational transmission of attachment patterns

(continued)

(continued)

Attachment theory & construct philosophy development timeline		
1992–1997	Crittenden develops lifespan attachment assessment tools	Crittenden develops several tools using qualitative and quantitative methods to understand the why underneath the behaviours
2006	The DMM is officially named	The DMM brings together all previous research with nuance and depth, acknowledging the complexity of human life
2008/2015	Crittenden's "Raising Parents" is published	"Raising Parents" is a seminal text for all professionals working with families, focusing on changing the danger and not the child
2013+	*Procter and Ugazio publish on family constructs*	*Brought family constructs to contemporary and wide audiences. Convergence of many elements of constructivism for the benefit of the family practitioner and clients*

Chapter 6
Beginning the Transformation from Theory to Practice

Now that we have covered the narratives of the creation of our theories and we now have knowledge of our integrated model of ICAT, our next step is to transform the philosophies and theories into practice. The following chapter will detail some key therapeutic techniques that shift the energy of our knowledge from something that we can observe to something we can work with for adaptive change. For any theory to be valid and clinically useful, we need evidence that our abstract thoughts are translatable to practice. The second part of this book will provide you with technical information as well as real-life case studies so that you can deepen your understanding. When I am training students and post-qualified professionals, they will often grasp the theories quickly and, just as quickly, follow this up with "why" and "how". The practical application of our knowledge will be laid out here, along with worksheets and ideas for working with children, adults and families in a range of settings. We are going to add three new theorists to our narrative who will provide key therapeutic techniques for the transformation of ICAT into practice. We will link up our knowledge so far before thinking about some more general techniques which are helpful for building trust in interpersonal relationships. Once we have covered these topics, we will explore case studies and real-life examples and models which will help you to find ways to apply ICAT to your own context. In this next section, I will use the term "psychic". In this, I am showing my own psychoanalytical roots, as by "psychic" I mean the emotional space and experience we create by being with another person… the feelings or the "vibes" (to use my children's turn of phrase). I will also use the term "mother" often. In some instances, I do mean parent or caregiver, or primary person. In other instances, I mean mother as in the person who gave birth to the infant, especially when we are talking about the biological changes and processes that occur in the mother–infant dyad. I often feel that one can't talk about families and parenting without thinking of one's own experiences, so sometimes I am even talking about me as a mother—especially as we think about being "good enough". So, let's get going again and meet Donald Winnicott.

R. Swanick, *A Clinical Guide to Interpersonal Constructs and Attachment Theory*, https://doi.org/10.1007/978-3-032-23728-6_6

Winnicott (1896–1971) was a highly influential British paediatrician and psychiatrist. When I first started my therapeutic training, it was Winnicott's work that made the most sense to me. He wrote in the most approachable way and even delivered regular radio programmes during the 1950s, where he would provide mothers with advice for guiding their children through their development. Winnicott wrote extensively on infant development and coined many key terms which have been integral to therapeutic work over the decades. I am going to concentrate on five terms here, linking them to attachment theory and interpersonal constructs as we explore them.

The Good Enough Mother

Winnicott was a member of the British Psychoanalytical Society at the same time as Bowlby, and although they remained separate as theorists, they were both champions of the importance of the mother in the mother–infant relationship. Winnicott famously said that "there is no such thing as a baby", meaning that the baby cannot exist in isolation and has to exist within a mother–infant relationship. The infant is born to the mother; the infant cannot survive without their mother (or caregiver). Interestingly, Winnicott did not call himself an attachment theorist and is noted outside of Bowlby's movement, but I can't untangle Winnicott's philosophies about mothers and infants from my knowledge of attachment theory. A criticism of many clinicians working with families is that there is often too much emphasis on what the mother does or does not do. As we saw with Bowlby and Ainsworth, this was not always the case, and so here, with Winnicott, who stated mothers should be "good enough". "The Good Enough Mother" (Winnicott, 1953) is not neglectful and rejecting, nor is she perfect and responding to every tiny inflexion; she is good enough. This means that she keeps the needs of her child in mind—she knows that he prefers the green cup, and doesn't like to mix his beans with his potatoes. She knows that her daughter likes to cuddle her before sleep and that the fairy tale with the wolf is her least favourite. Most of the time, 75% of the time, a mother gets it right for her children. When parenting doesn't go according to plan, the mother can reflect and repair with her child, and they go on being in this supportive way.

When I first read about being good enough, I felt a huge wave of relief. I was training to be a therapist, and I had not had my own children, and I felt I could be human and authentic in my therapeutic alliances. When we think about the transitional attachment figure (Crittenden, 2015) and the more knowledgeable other (Vygotsky, 1978), we can transpose the dynamics of the mother–infant into our professional relationships. If we are working with a client or a student who needs support, we can be good enough for them. We can keep their needs in mind as much as possible, responding in an appropriate way 75% of the time so that the client or student can internalise those interpersonal constructs for future use. If we are too perfect, then the individual may not build any resilience, as they will not have experienced mistakes and reparation, integral to healthy development. If we do not keep their needs in mind, we risk colluding with maladaptive patterns of attachment and perpetuating feelings of distress in the individual. By being "the good enough mother as a transitional attachment figure", we give the individual a new way of being in their relationships, which promotes co-operation, nurture, and humanness.

The Transitional Object

We briefly touched on the transitional object in our work on Crittenden earlier, and we have discussed it above. So, let's explore this more deeply, now. The transitional object serves as a bridge during the process of individuation (becoming separate). This is an important stage of development, underscored by Winnicott's quote on the baby, which we must keep in our minds. When a mother gives birth to their infant, they certainly does feel like the same organism. The mother's brain actively changes to accommodate the needs of their baby very intensely. The amygdala, which is responsible for threat detection, grows in volume so that the mother can protect their child, whilst the brain area responsible for reward recognition also grows, making it more possible for the mother to interact with their infant in a rewarding way; do you remember Bowlby saying that it is important for mothers to feel positive reciprocity in their infant relationship? (Barba-Muller et al., 2019). Once the need for this intense connection has reduced, usually when the infant begins to eat finger foods, or begins to notice different caregivers around them, both mother and infant realise they are separate with different needs. For both parent and child, there is a grief associated with this time as well as an excitement as the world starts to open up. The intense closeness of infancy takes up a lot of energy and parental capacity, and the infant has only trusted their main caregiver thus far in their short lives. Both know, however, that we can't stop the tide and that a temporary measure is needed to help the transition from infancy to childhood. For many children, the transitional object is a dummy or a blanket, and I have known many adults who still have their transitional objects in a box in the loft (or secretly under their pillows). The mother instills their psychic love into the object, and the child can take it with them to nursery or school or to Granny's house, knowing that their mother loves them and will return. Soon enough, the child will become more interested in the world around them—friends, secure relationships with grandparents and teachers—and as they have internalised their parents' love, the transitional object becomes a sacred and yet unused object. This is right and just.

In our professional relationships, we see this in how our clients and students relate to us. They come to depend on us for advice for many months and sessions, before gaining their confidence in their own feelings and instincts or finding a trusted friend or partner who supports them. We may even see the use of transitional objects—perhaps a family member brings a child with their special object, handing both over to us with care, or maybe we give a special toy from our therapy bag to the child to take home so they can bring it back next week. In each case, this will only happen for as long as the child or person needs it. There is a beauty and a grief in the moment they decide they don't need us or our toys anymore, just like the mother and infant.

The Holding Environment

Winnicott's "holding environment" first begins as a physical action when the mother holds the baby in their arms to help the baby feel safe and settled. As we grow, we often return to this feeling when we seek hugs and closeness from those whom we trust. The holding environment moves from being a physical and emotional one to a psychic and emotional one. As we have seen through attachment theory and constructivism, we each have to internalise an experience or feeling repeatedly before we can externalise the behaviours related to that experience or feeling. This is the same for the holding environment: we need to internalise the safety of being physically held before we can create and use the psychic space in later development.

As the mother's brain actively changes during pregnancy and early infancy (and for up to 2 years after birth, although I feel certain my brain has never again functioned as it did before childbirth!), the mother becomes more sensitive to the infant's needs. Ainsworth (Ainsworth et al., 1956) called this "maternal sensitivity", and Winnicott called this "primary maternal preoccupation" (PMP, Winnicott, 1956). PMP is the intrapsychic process whereby the mother keeps the infant's needs in mind and becomes a good enough mother. The mother uses this sensory and emotional input to respond positively to the infant through physical holding, helping to build secure dispositional representations for an attachment figure. The mother then moves this physical holding to emotional holding—responding promptly when the infant cries, ensuring the food is at the right temperature to be devoured when hungry, etc. As the infant moves through childhood, the mother tactically "fails" so that the child builds resilience and can wait with security. For instance, the food make take five more minutes to arrive at the table, or the mother may say "let me finish this and then I will play with you". This encourages the child to build trust.

When we think of professional relationships, the holding environment remains firmly in the psychic and emotional space. The therapist, for instance, will arrange therapy at the same time, in the same place, with the same chair, so that the client is kept in mind and can trust everything will be the same. When everything is the same, we can reduce our fears, as we know our brains are economical machines and like to predict everything will be as it always was. Furthermore, if the therapeutic space remains the same, the client relaxes, and they can show their true self (see below), taking away defences and enabling a place where positive change can happen. Later in Part II, I will describe how the holding environment can be used in therapy and in the workplace through some case studies.

Play

For Winnicott, play was the foundation for healthy development and a way to discover the "true self" (see below), in that an individual needs to feel truly free to be creative. Winnicott's definition of play is that structureless, spontaneous play that happens when we are without rules or constraints. He connected play with feeling alive, and a place which is both exciting and precarious as we test what is real and what is in our minds through the act of play. The child first explores play with the transitional object, perhaps practising the feeling of when the mother returns. In fact, the psychic space where play happens is often called the "potential space", and the child can scrutinise what is "me" and what is "not me" (Winnicott, 1971). Once the child has internalised this moment, they then move on to playing alone and then with others. Play continues into adulthood, where we engage in hobbies, culture, religion, and any type of research.

Play can only genuinely happen in a safe place, when we feel emotionally and physically safe, as in the holding environment (above). In our professional work, the individuals who are referred to us will often be coming to our spaces whilst in crisis and in distress, and therefore feeling unsafe. The first goal of any professional interpersonal relationship is to create this safe holding environment so that the individual can reveal their true self through play—whether that be a creative activity, a shared experience or a sense of freedom in their verbal responses.

The True and False Self

Our final Winnicott concept here is the "true and false self". Winnicott's definition is not concerned with good or bad here; it is about safety, and is similar to when we think about Crittenden's proposal that all attachment behaviours have an underlying function to seek safety. The false self is a defensive stance that we create to help us feel safe. It masks our true feelings so that we can go under the radar or act in a way that protects our vulnerabilities. These defensive strategies arise in our early attachment relationships—perhaps the caregiver did not respond in a good enough way—and are deeply linked to attachment theory, even though Winnicott never explicitly states this. Our true self is when we can feel vulnerable or switch off our anxious brains and really engage in the moment. It appears in play, in safe relationships and when we really feel like ourselves. As with the DMM, the true and false self can be adaptive and maladaptive; something we do in a specific context that helps us to feel safe, but becomes unsafe in another context.

In professional situations, it can be the client who feels empty or the client you find hard to respond to. In school, it can be the student who smiles but not with their eyes and who wants to please intensely. At work, it might be the person who completes all of the tasks but does not engage with their co-workers. In contemporary culture, the false self could be the social media posts we see of perfect families vs.

the posts we see of chaotic lifestyles. It is important to say that the false self is adaptive, and it has a place. We have to have defences in order to function. Imagine if we were completely open and vulnerable at work—we would never get anything done, especially if we are therapists. Still, we have to have places where our true selves can shine. That might be on our own in our hobbies and interests, or with people we love and trust. It can happen in our therapy, educational and work places when we create a meaningful boundary.

Within the interpersonal constructs and attachment theory (ICAT) framework, Winnicott's concepts can be understood as early relational mechanisms through which attachment strategies and interpersonal constructs are co-formed and revised. From an ICAT perspective, the "good enough mother" represents the original relational context in which a child's dispositional representations and meaning-making systems are shaped—not through perfection, but through consistent attunement, rupture, and repair. These repeated relational experiences enable the child to internalise expectations of safety, responsiveness, and co-operation, forming both attachment strategies and core interpersonal constructs that guide future anticipation and behaviour. Transitional objects and holding environments function as relational bridges, allowing the individual to move between dependence and autonomy while maintaining psychological continuity; in ICAT terms, they support the gradual shift from externally scaffolded regulation to internally-held constructs of safety and trust. Play emerges as the experiential space in which these constructs are tested, revised, and creatively expanded, requiring sufficient attachment security to allow exploration without collapse. The distinction between the true and the false self further aligns with ICAT's emphasis on adaptive self-protective strategies: the false self reflects context-specific attachment and construct strategies designed to maintain safety, while the true self becomes accessible only within relationships and environments that support affect attunement, mentalisation, and reflective flexibility—concepts we will now think through together, beginning with our next contributor, Daniel Stern.

Stern (1932–2012) was an American psychologist and psychiatrist who revolutionised how professionals thought about mother–infant relationships. If Winnicott provided our holding environment, Stern provided a "micro-map" which details the series of tiny interactions which build a shared experience in the mother–infant relationship. Stern was another professional who pushed against the traditional forms of psychoanalysis, which concentrated on "macro" events such as depression or anxiety. Instead, Stern used 16 mm film to record the micro events (eye gaze, silences, and so on) that actually build a child's internal world (Beebe, 2017). Through the analysis of these recordings, Stern noticed that the infant was not passive and was actively seeking sensation and connection to be involved in the interpersonal relationship. Once the sensations were felt in the infant, they would become connected to another sensation and then another, leading to a set of behaviours and expectations. Stern proposed his own stages of development, which you can read about in his book, The Interpersonal World of the Infant (1985). We are going to think about Representations of Interactions that have been Generalised RIGs, the intersubjective self, and most importantly, affect attunement, here.

Representations of Interactions That Have Been Generalised (RIGs)

Stern believed that RIGs are the foundational building blocks of a human's internal world, which are created from thousands of micro events that occur in every interaction. A RIG is a summary of several micro events, rather than a single memory (Stern, 1985):

- The Episode: A baby has a specific interaction (perhaps they cry, the mother picks them up and hums a specific tune).
- The Invariant: The baby's brain looks for what stays the same across different versions of this event—the "islands of consistency".
- The Generalisation: After many such moments, the baby creates a RIG: a mental "script" that says, *"When I am distressed and make this sound, a comforting presence arrives with this rhythm"*.

Stern described RIGs as "islands of consistency", perhaps meaning that they become core memories for the infant as they initiate their sense of self. RIGs enable the infant to predict feelings based on previous experiences, as well as providing a way for the infant to share experiences with their caregiver as they "remember" the patterns of their interactions. A RIG is a form of procedural memory, or to put it in Crittenden's words, the knowledge of how to be with another person (1990). So far, this could sound remarkably like Internal Working Models, Dispositional Representations and Constructs. However, it is the specific nature of Stern's observations that highlights the differences. The table below compares Stern with Bowlby and Crittenden.

When we review the information in Table 6.1, we can see how Stern focuses on the *feeling* rather than the strategic use of the behaviour, as in Bowlby and Crittenden. Rather than thinking about the event as a whole, whatever that may be, in Stern's

Table 6.1 Descriptors and comparisons of Stern, Bowlby, and Crittenden's internal concepts. Author's own

Feature	Stern's RIGs	Bowlby's IWM	Crittenden's DRs
Full name	Representations of Interactions that have been Generalised	Internal Working Model	Dispositional Representations
"Zoom" level	Microscopic: The split-second rhythm and "music" of a hug.	Macroscopic: The overall reliability of a caregiver.	Strategic: The "if/then" shortcuts for surviving danger.
Focus	Vitality & Being: How it *feels* to be with another.	Security & Prediction: Can I trust this person?	Survival & Info-Processing: How must I act to stay safe?
Memory type	Implicit/Procedural (non-verbal).	Cognitive/Reflective "Template."	Multi-system (Procedural, Imaged, Semantic, Episodic).

theory, the focal point is on the micro shifts in nonverbal communication that build our sense of self in relation to another person.

So, how do we do this, how do we actually respond to the infant in such a way that they can internalise feelings, holding, empathy, and security? Through the analysis of mother–infant recordings, Stern noticed how the mother responds to the infant in those moments of connection. He found that the mother would tune into, or attune, the nonverbal and verbal communication of the infant, matching and mirroring the infant's reactions. Stern labelled this affect attunement; the attunement to the emotional affects. We will have seen this act many times and perhaps not even paid it much attention. It is the moment when the baby cries, and the mother moves to the infant, perhaps picking them up, matching the expressions of the infant and saying, "Oh! What's to do! Do you need some food?". We can link this to another Winnicottian term, the Ordinary Devoted Mother (1956), highlighting that parents everywhere do this in every interaction. By responding in this emotive way, the mother matches the intensity of the infant, giving them a sense of being seen and heard, and continues the act by responding to the need, building those internal blocks of secure attachment with her ordinary behaviours.

We can go further with this exploration—when the mother responds to the infant's emotions, they are responding to the infant's vitality affects. Stern likened vitality affects in humans to musical patterns—they are the rhythm, melody and pulse of how we move and express ourselves. Stern categorised our vitality affects, suggesting the most common to be:

- Surging—a sudden rush of excitement
- Fading—a slow loss of energy
- Explosive—a sharp burst
- Fleeting—a quick light touch
- Drawn-out—a steady lingering tension

If we go back to our mother attuning to her infant when they cried, above, we can imagine the mother rocking the baby in a steady pulse to calm them, or using her voice in a similar pitch to the infant's cries. Therefore, we can say that the mother attunes to the vitality affects of her infant to help relieve their distress. She responds to the energy and acknowledges the feeling in the infant's externalisations. By using affect attunement and understanding the importance of vitality affects in our professional work, we can help our clients and students to feel seen and, again, internalise the sense of being listened to. In work with children, we can match their energy and intensity instead of negating their feelings by asking them to "calm down". When working with adults, therapeutically, educationally or in management, we can still find ways to meet their feelings by responding with facial expressions and similar intonation. We can also notice when their vitality affects change, with the classic example being when someone says they are fine, and yet their body language tells a different story. Again, we are reminded of the imperative nature of interpersonal relationships when shaping our sense of self and our emotional worlds.

Once the infant or individual has experienced positive affect attunement with another person, they can move towards a shared emotional experience called

Intersubjectivity. This is a transformational process where we realise that we are not the only one who feels this feeling, it is a shared one. It begins with those early moments of affect attunement, moves to shared attention (both looking at the dog in the park, for instance), and continues towards shared agreements and the ability to co-operate and empathise with another. For the infant, intersubjectivity opens the world further, and for the developing child and adult, it becomes a cornerstone of successful and reciprocal interpersonal relationships. If a key element of attachment theory is that it is prosocial, having an intersubjective understanding of the experience of another person helps us to know how to look after them, support them with their experiences and provide guidance when needed. We can only truly have this awareness when we feel safe with another, as we have to feel safe enough to explore the imagined feelings of another and express ourselves. When we do feel safe, and the experience does become shared, we can feel resonances with another, building stronger and deeper interpersonal connections—and change can happen. If we think professionally here, we can help our clients, students and staff to feel safe by attuning to their affects, meeting their needs, acknowledging this out loud and encouraging them to notice that their experience is shared. In turn, the client, student or staff member trusts us and verbalises their concerns where we can co-create solutions to foster positive change for them.

Within the ICAT framework, Stern's work provides a crucial micro-process account of how attachment strategies and interpersonal constructs are first formed through lived, moment-to-moment relational experience. His concepts of Representations of Interactions that have been Generalised (RIGs), affect attunement, vitality affects, and intersubjectivity illuminate how repeated micro-interactions—eye contact, rhythm, tone, movement, and timing—become internalised as procedural knowledge about how it feels to be with another. From an ICAT perspective, RIGs can be understood as the embodied precursors to Internal Working Models, Dispositional Representations, and Interpersonal Constructs: they are not abstract beliefs, but felt expectations that organise anticipation, emotional regulation, and relational behaviour. Affect attunement functions as the relational mechanism through which safety, meaning, and emotional coherence are co-created, enabling the individual to move from isolated experience toward shared understanding and co-operation. Intersubjectivity, in turn, represents the developmental outcome of successful attunement, supporting prosocial functioning, mentalisation, and flexible meaning-making across the lifespan. Together, Stern's contributions ground ICAT in the embodied, relational present, demonstrating that attachment and construct processes are continually shaped through micro-level interactions and offering a powerful bridge between early developmental experience and contemporary therapeutic, educational, and organisational practice.

I would like to take a side step and acknowledge that I am bouncing around with theories, whereas in Part One, we had a lovely, straight narrative. However, we have the luxury of time in our contemporary place. We can view all that has been before us and find a golden thread as to where we are now. We can also see how each theorist before us has deepened our knowledge so that, in the here and now, we have a chance to fully utilise all that has been before us. In Part II, we have

Winnicott's Good Enough Mother and the Ordinary Devoted Mother who attends to their infant in a natural and responsive way. With Stern, we can see that she did this through Affect Attunement and by matching the infant's vitality affects. We have even transposed these ideas into our professional practice—and by the end of this book, you will fully have the skills to do this. So now, let us go even further into our theoretical adventure and think about how the mother knows what affects to attune to; how they know what the infant needs in those microevents and in the holding environment. May I introduce you to Peter Fonagy and Mentalisation.

Fonagy (b.1952) is a leading British Psychoanalyst and Clinical Psychologist who has brought incredible depth to professional knowledge on how humans relate and understand themselves and each other. To review where we have been so far in this chapter, Winnicott brought us a sense of safety in the holding environment, Stern brought us a sense of being seen with all our emotions, and Fonagy will now bring us a sense of being understood through the therapeutic term of Mentalisation (Fonagy et al., 2002). This theory is around knowing we feel and think, whilst knowing what others feel and think. In this definition, mentalisation sounds a lot like Dispositional Representations, Affect Attunement and Constructivist theories. However, mentalisation adds the energy of flexibility to these earlier theories, enabling us to not only have strategies for safety and labels for categorisation, but to imagine a narrative behind the feelings we are perceiving so that we can fully understand them. Let's look at some examples.

Mentalisation Versus Dispositional Representations (DRs)

- The Difference: A DR is a "shortcut" to keep you safe from a parent or partner. It is often unconscious and rigid: *"I must always smile to keep them happy"*.
- Mentalisation is the ability to *step back* from that DR and think: *"I feel like I have to smile, but actually, my partner is just tired, they aren't actually angry at me"*.
- Key: Mentalisation breaks the rigid grip of a DR.

Mentalisation Versus Affect Attunement

- The Difference: Attunement is non-verbal and "in the moment". It's about the *feeling*; the "vitality affect".
- Mentalisation goes a step further by adding meaning.
- Example: A mother attunes to a baby's cry by humming sadly (Stern). She mentalises the baby by thinking, *"He's crying because he's frustrated that the toy broke"* (Fonagy). Attunement is the *resonance*; mentalisation is the *interpretation*.

Mentalisation Versus Interpersonal Constructs

- The Difference: A Construct is a "box" we put people in ("Teachers are strict"; "Men are dangerous"). It helps us predict the world.
- Mentalisation is the "flexibility" of those boxes.
- Example: If you have a construct that "Bosses are mean," and your boss is quiet one day, a Construct user might just say "See, they're being mean/cold." A Mentaliser would think, *"Maybe they're quiet because they had a bad morning, not because they are being 'mean' in the way I expect"*.

These are simplified examples to show the differences between the theories, and I truly believe that flexibility is possible in all stances, be that DRs, constructs, etc. We can use the examples to understand how mentalisation brings meaning and colour, creating an imaginative back story to the experiences we are having. Fonagy suggested that mentalisation is the "psychological immune system", meaning that when we are able to think about our cause and effect, as well as that of the other, we can protect ourselves from emotional harm. We can justify what is happening and why; we are reasoning with the emotional senses we are feeling.

As with all of our theories and philosophies detailed in this book, mentalisation also starts in those early interactions between parent and infant. If we imagine an infant crying, the parent uses affect attunement to mirror or match those feelings, and with the process of mentalisation, they psychically remove themselves from the attunement by noticing that it is the infant who is sad and not themselves. Once they have separated their feeling from the infants, they can then acknowledge the infants unique experience of feeling sad verbally or gesturally, so that infant begins to know their sad feelings. As the parent acknowledges the feelings in a "marked" or exaggerated/external way, the infant builds up an experience of knowing it is okay to feel sad because their parent sees that and can hold it for them. Fonagy called this destination the "psychological self", which is a place where we know our own minds and feelings. We can then link this to attachment theory in that once we have built our psychological self and we can mentalise our feelings, we can be prosocial and support others to know their feelings, continuing a positive feedback loop. We know how it feels to be understood, so we can help others to do so, too.

In professional application, mentalisation can be used to help our clients, students and staff to think about thinking. By using our experiences in the here-and-now of a safe space, we can help our clients to be aware of how they process things. For example, a client may become defensive after he notices his therapist checking their watch partway through the session. The therapist can notice this and talk about it with the client, asking if they have noticed the feeling and what it might mean. Another example may be when working with mothers with postnatal depression and their infants. The therapist or professional may offer observations of how the infant may be feeling, verbalising proposed feelings and thoughts of the infant and the mother, so that they can know and understand their feelings.

Within the ICAT framework, Fonagy's theory of mentalisation provides a crucial integrative bridge between attachment processes, interpersonal constructs, and lived relational experience by introducing psychological flexibility as a core mechanism of change. While Dispositional Representations, Affect Attunement, and Constructs describe how individuals anticipate, feel, and categorise relational experience in order to remain safe, mentalisation enables a reflective stance toward these processes, allowing the individual to step back from rigid self-protective strategies and consider the intentions, feelings, and perspectives of both self and other. Mentalisation transforms resonance into meaning and prediction into curiosity, supporting the development of a coherent psychological self that can tolerate emotional complexity without collapse. From an attachment perspective, this capacity emerges through early caregiving relationships in which the child's emotional experience is both attuned to and meaningfully reflected, fostering prosocial functioning and empathic understanding across development. In ICAT terms, mentalisation represents the mechanism through which attachment strategies and interpersonal constructs become open to revision, enabling individuals to move from automatic relational loops toward conscious, shared meaning-making. This capacity is therefore central to therapeutic, educational, and organisational practice, as it allows professionals to create relational spaces where thinking about thinking becomes possible, setting the foundation for the applied interventions and clinical work explored in the next section of this book.

From Relational Foundations to Transformative Practice

Across this section, we have traced a developmental and relational arc that deepens our understanding of how safety, meaning, and understanding emerge within human relationships. Winnicott's contributions foregrounded the necessity of a sufficiently safe relational environment in which development can unfold. Through the concepts of the Good Enough Mother, the holding environment, transitional objects, play, and the true and false self, he demonstrated that psychological growth does not depend on perfection, but on reliable attunement, rupture, and repair. These early relational experiences allow the infant—and later the child and adult—to internalise safety, tolerate frustration, and develop resilience, creating the conditions under which authenticity and creativity can emerge.

Stern extended this foundation by illuminating the *micro-processes* through which such safety and meaning are actually built. His focus on moment-to-moment interaction revealed that infants are active participants in relational life, continually organising experience through patterns of sensation, rhythm, and affect. Representations of Interactions that have been Generalised (RIGs), vitality affects, affect attunement, and intersubjectivity demonstrate how repeated micro-interactions become internalised as procedural knowledge about how it feels to be with another. In doing so, Stern showed that relational meaning is not constructed retrospectively through narrative alone, but is embodied, rhythmic, and emotionally alive in the present moment.

Fonagy's theory of mentalisation then added a further dimension by articulating how individuals come not only to feel and anticipate relational experience, but to *understand* it. Mentalisation enables a reflective stance toward one's own internal states and those of others, introducing flexibility into systems that might otherwise become rigidly organised around safety. By supporting the development of a psychological self—one that can recognise feelings as mental states rather than overwhelming realities—mentalisation allows individuals to move from automatic self-protective strategies toward curiosity, empathy, and shared meaning. Importantly, this capacity is rooted in early caregiving relationships in which affect is both attuned to and meaningfully reflected, reinforcing the prosocial nature of attachment across the lifespan.

Together, these theorists offer a richly layered account of relational development: from the establishment of safety, to the experience of being seen, and finally to the capacity to be understood. Each perspective deepens the last, moving from environmental holding to embodied interaction to reflective awareness, and each has profound implications for therapeutic, educational, and organisational practice.

Situating These Contributions Within ICAT

Within the Interpersonal Constructs and Attachment Theory (ICAT) framework, the work of Winnicott, Stern, and Fonagy can be understood as describing complementary layers of the same relational system through which attachment strategies and interpersonal constructs are formed, maintained, and revised. Winnicott elucidates the conditions of safety required for interpersonal constructs and attachment strategies to emerge without collapse; Stern reveals the micro-level relational processes through which these constructs are embodied and proceduralised; and Fonagy articulates the reflective capacity through which such constructs and strategies become open to examination and change. ICAT integrates these perspectives by recognising that attachment strategies, Dispositional Representations, Interpersonal Constructs, affective processes, and Mentalisation are not separate mechanisms, but interdependent functions within a dynamic relational loop. Meaning is constructed through interaction, safety is negotiated through relationship, and change becomes possible when individuals are supported to reflect on how they anticipate, feel, and interpret interpersonal experience. This integrated understanding provides the conceptual foundation for the applied work that follows, where ICAT will be translated into concrete therapeutic, educational, and organisational practices aimed at fostering flexibility, resilience, and meaningful relational change.

Part II
The Application of ICAT: Interpersonal Constructs and Attachment Theory

Change occurs not through insight alone, but through repeated experiences of regulated, meaningful, and ethically-held relationships.

1.1 Introduction

Welcome to Part II of our attachment theory and interpersonal construct journey. We are going to take all of the knowledge we have gathered in Part I and transpose this into our clinical practice. To slightly misquote William Morris, we need our professional knowledge to be beautiful and practical, and as we have completed our beautiful philosophical journey, we now need to find a way for our knowledge to become useful and practical. I am going to mainly use the term "practitioner" to indicate the therapist, educator, manager, or person of professional responsibility, and the term "individual" to indicate we are talking about the client, student, staff member, or person who has been referred.

Chapter 7
From Theory to Practice: Introducing ICAT in Applied Contexts

Part I of this book traced the theoretical and philosophical foundations underpinning the Interpersonal Constructs and Attachment Theory (ICAT) model, bringing together attachment theory, constructivist and constructionist traditions, and personal and systemic construct psychology. Across these chapters, the focus has been on understanding how human beings develop expectations of self and others, regulate emotion, construct meaning, and navigate relationships within specific relational, cultural, and developmental contexts. Rather than treating these theories as discrete or competing frameworks, Part I has demonstrated their conceptual convergence around a shared concern with relational experience, anticipation, safety, and change.

Beginning with classical and contemporary attachment theory, Part I explored how early caregiving relationships shape internal working models, dispositional representations, and attachment strategies that guide perception, affect regulation, and behaviour across the lifespan. These processes were situated within broader developmental and ecological systems, drawing particularly on the Dynamic-Maturational Model to highlight how attachment strategies are adaptive responses to perceived danger rather than fixed traits or deficits. This emphasis on function over pathology provided a critical lens through which later theories could be integrated.

Constructivist and constructionist perspectives were then introduced to extend attachment theory beyond behaviour and emotion into the domain of meaning-making. From Piaget and Vygotsky's accounts of cognitive and social development, through Papert's constructionism and Berger and Luckmann's social constructionism, knowledge was reframed as actively constructed through interaction, language, culture, and power. George Kelly's personal construct psychology offered a pivotal bridge between these traditions and attachment theory, conceptualising individuals as active meaning-makers who anticipate events through internally organised, relationally derived constructs. Subsequent developments in systemic and family construct psychology further demonstrated how meaning is co-constructed within

R. Swanick, *A Clinical Guide to Interpersonal Constructs and Attachment Theory*, https://doi.org/10.1007/978-3-032-23728-6_7

relational systems, reinforcing or constraining individual experience through shared narratives and interactional patterns.

The later chapters of Part I brought these strands into closer dialogue through the work of Winnicott, Stern, and Fonagy. Winnicott's concepts of the good enough caregiver, the holding environment, transitional phenomena, play, and the true and false self illustrated how safety and relational reliability create the conditions for exploration and authenticity. Stern's micro-analytic work on affect attunement, vitality affects, RIGs, and intersubjectivity grounded attachment and construct processes in moment-to-moment embodied interaction, demonstrating how expectations and relational knowledge are formed through repeated micro-events. Fonagy's theory of mentalisation added a crucial dimension of psychological flexibility and illuminated the ways in which individuals come to understand their own and others' minds and how reflective capacity enables movement beyond rigid self-protective strategies.

Together, I have synthesised these theories into the ICAT model, which conceptualises human functioning as an ongoing interplay between attachment strategies, interpersonal constructs, affective experience, and reflective meaning-making. ICAT proposes that behaviour, emotion, and cognition are best understood as relationally organised responses to safety, danger, and context, and that change becomes possible when relational conditions support attunement, mentalisation, and flexible reconstruing. Importantly, Part I also highlighted the limits of these processes, acknowledging the roles of neurobiology, culture, trauma, and power in shaping when and how relational change can occur.

This theoretical foundation sets the stage for Part II, which shifts the focus from understanding to application. Having established how attachment and constructs are formed, maintained, and revised, we turn to the practical question of how practitioners can work ethically and effectively within these frameworks. Part II will explore how ICAT can be translated into clinical, educational, and organisational practice, examining both the techniques that support relational change and the contexts in which such work must be adapted, slowed, or deferred. In doing so, the book moves from theory as explanation to theory as guide, offering a relationally grounded approach to practice that is attuned to safety, difference, and the lived realities of those we seek to support.

ICAT is a *dynamic process*, not an intervention

When we think about the professional application of ICAT, we need to note that it is a dynamic observation and thought process and not a strict intervention. With this in mind, the ethos for ICAT is "what does this relational system need right now to make thinking possible?" By referring back to this ethos and reminding ourselves why we are working in this way, we can keep our focus on supporting the clients, students and staff (I will refer to these various groups as individuals going forward). ICAT, by definition, is a philosophy and a theory. Using the frame of interpersonal constructs, we can think about what internal representations the individuals we are working with are using as a basis for their actions and reactions. By exploring this framework with them, we can begin to understand their experiences and how they are playing out in the here and now. For example, perhaps a staff member is struggling to be in a leadership role and by thinking about their past experiences, we can see that in their home life, they have felt oppressed. A student, perhaps, may need lots of attention in school because there is some neglect at home. By exploring the interpersonal constructs of the individual—within the boundaries of our professional roles—we can gain information on how we can support them in the present.

If you are worried about neglect or abuse, or something which you cannot support in your professional duties, always consult a safeguarding lead. The ICAT is here to help you with what you can legitimately do n in your daily routines.

We can, subsequently, transform the information gleaned in the professional experience with the use of attachment theory by essentially "giving the best of ourselves" to support the individual (Crittenden, 2015). We can attune to the individual in a gentle way, acknowledging some of the feelings being held. We can interpret those feelings and give them names, responding to the need for safety of the individual. Often, when individuals are feeling stressed, they will anticipate the worst in others and expect that there isn't a solution. As we have seen in the theories of dispositional representations and constructs, if an individual is feeling unsafe, the impact of their anticipation can be overwhelming. Therefore, by us as practitioners making space for safety and reflection—even in busy schools, clinics and offices—we can help those we work with to engage in our contexts in a more positive way.

The Practitioner as a Relational Participant

To really meet the individual and their needs, we can become the Transitional Attachment Figure (TAF) in the professional context. As described in Part I, the TAF has the opportunity to provide a positive relationship for the individual whilst there is a specific need. The TAF can represent a mirror or a thinking person to the individual, providing the secure attributes of an attachment figure in a professional way. The TAF is different to the "Resilient Other" and the "Alternative Attachment Figure" (Zaccagnino et al., 2014), who is often a family member or trusted friend. A resilient other will provide safety through a good enough holding environment and the use of affect attunement, and they will do this in an ordinary, caring way. The TAF is a conscious process with an ending aim. The relationship is based on theory and knowledge, and by the end of the intervention, the individual should have felt some resolution. As with the resilient other, the TAF provides a holding space where the individual feels safe enough to explore their feelings accurately through attunement—if we remember from the DMM, when we feel attacked or that we have to defend ourselves, we often omit or distort information to adapt to the situation. The holding space here, then, aims to provide a place where the individual can acknowledge what has been too difficult to feel so that it can be thought about with the TAF. Once the information is in the consciousness of the individual, it can be related to the "facts" of the situation and the crisis may feel reduced. For example, if an individual is presenting with avoidant attachment strategies, the TAF will need to be warm and expressive so that trust can be built. If the individual is more ambivalent, consistency and structure are important so that they can bring the opposing sides of their feelings together. We can say that the role of the TAF is to provide protection in the safe holding space; information processing—helping the individual to feel and know the omitted/distorted information; and then integration—helping the individual to link their feelings to facts in order to see the whole situation from a balanced perspective.

We have discussed Vygotksy's idea of the More Knowledgeable Other (MKO) and, at first sight, this feels akin to the Transitional Attachment Figure. Some theorists feel that the main difference between MKO and TAF is that of context. As Vygotsky's work is situated in Learning Theory, the MKO provides the individual with an opportunity to learn a specific skill in an educational environment. The learning takes place in the individual's Zone of Proximal Development, the "sweet spot" where the learner feels positively challenged. Perhaps this could be the skill to revise well or to master algebra. The MKO can be any other individual who has the skills to share—be that a teenager helping their grandparent with social media, or a trusted older supervisor supporting a young trainee. Whilst this definition of the MKO is true, I think we can use Kelly's definition of each of us bringing our own views of reality and make a clearer link to attachment theory through Vygotsky. In the early experiences of the infant, and through childhood, the parent is the MKO, providing emotional, practical and physical support to guide and educate the child. This learning happens in the Zone of Proximal Development as a psychic space, when the child is ready to engage. As the child grows through adolescence, a time when peer relationships become paramount, the MKO may be a friend or family member outside of the home, offering an opportunity to widen viewpoints of how people live differently and providing affirmation or challenge as needed. Interestingly, the MKO may not be able to function in the interpersonal space with a sense of emotional safety, as the individual may not feel able to bring their true selves to the ZPD, and this sense of safety feels like a key element of the TAF. Therefore, when we are working professionally, there is space to be both the Transitional Attachment Figure to someone and the More Knowledgeable Other in ways that are connected and distinct. We bring emotional safety to that connection that can be created in the interpersonal relationship, and then we use the psychic space of the Zone of Proximal Development to be the More Knowledgeable Other, offering much-needed skills to the individual at a time when they need them and are ready to engage.

Ethical Implications—Power

When we hold the role of Transitional Attachment Figure (TAF), More Knowledgeable Other (MKO) or even as a therapist, educator or manager, we have to think about power. In my many years of experience as a manager and supervisor, I have found that people find it hard to name and think about power imbalances. It feels tricky and produces a visceral reaction, often. Interestingly, I have noticed it is sometimes easier for staff and therapists to talk about being the vulnerable person in a power dynamic, rather than admitting they hold the power. We will want our relationships—professional and personal—to feel equal and collaborative, but the influence of power through choice, free will and intensity of need will prevail. Our interpersonal constructs and attachment experiences will dictate how we react in those moments—what does it feel like to be in charge, how does it feel to be given advice from a man when you are woman, what does it feel like as a person of colour to be supported by a white person, what does it feel like being told what to do by anyone, full stop? Our early relationships of being parented, being at school, and making friends will colour how we manage and think about power.

I have a personal interest in gender power and how societal expectations of women and the dominant patriarchal systems have shaped (women's) personalities and expectations of behaviour. You will bring your own lens onto power, whether that be your age, your race and culture, your physical and cognitive abilities, so it is worth exploring your own shadows and edges as to where you can think about power in your own life.

Before an individual attends therapy, school or work, there is a power imbalance in that the constraints of time and place will have been set without including the individual. Sure, in therapy and sometimes in work, we may have some flexibility, and there could be options for when we attend, for example. However, the amount of time expected and even the options offered by the workplace are often suggested with the need of the therapist or manager in mind—rather than the client or employee. The sense of power through choice is almost an illusion here. It reminds me of when I offer dinner to my children, I will say, "What would you like—chicken or fish?", giving them a sense of choice whilst fulfilling my own needs of only making chicken or fish, as that is what I have available. Foucault stated that power is only tolerable if part of it is masked (1978, p. 86). If we think of the examples above, we can see that power is indeed masked, and then it becomes acceptable, perhaps even co-created or collaborative. The manager gives the staff an option, and the staff choose to buy into that dynamic through selecting an option offered. The power is not absolute from the manager as this would be dictatorship or abuse but it is limited so that the relationship and the business, in this instance, can function.

So how does this relate to the TAF and the MKO? When we work in these roles with our clients, staff and students, the power imbalance is greater than in our "normal" professional relationships. Firstly, we have the setting of times and venues, as above. Then, whereas in a working therapeutic or work relationship we might co-create aims and objectives, the TAF and MKO are recruited to complete a specific aim due to their skill set. The aims, the process, and the definition of the names of these roles mean that the practitioner is holding more power than the individual, and this needs to be carefully thought about. Whether you take Voltaire or Spiderman's view, with great power comes great responsibility in the underlying feeling in the interpersonal relationship between the individual and TAF or MKO. When we seek support from this kind of relationship, we are saying that we have reached the edge of our skill set or that we are in crisis and don't know what to do next. We put the power implicitly into the hands of another to "fix" our issues. If it works out and we feel better, then we can be eternally grateful to them. If it doesn't, then we can blame them and perhaps soothe ourselves with the thought that we are not the problem. Whether the relationship goes well or not, we still have to reflect on the difficulties that may arise.

To support someone to address their dispositional representations, interpersonal constructs, or to feel safe to make mistakes in their learning and work means that we as practitioners have to create safety. We have seen over the many decades of theory covered throughout Part I that the pathway to secure and positive life experiences is feeling safe, and we do this through meaningful emotional connection. We can go back to Crittenden, "how do we bring the best of ourselves to the work?". Of course, we can only do this by being genuine, by caring for the individuals we work with and the outcomes we wish to achieve. The individual will feel heard and seen, perhaps on one of the first few times in their life. We will feel listened to and like the expert (perhaps also for the first time) and the power completely tips to us. The individual may become dependent on our advice, coming to us for every decision. We might react to this by encouraging the longevity of the work with more sessions or answering emails and calls outside of the allocated times. Alternatively, the individual may become resentful of us for knowing all of the answers or remaining boundaried and not answering calls outside of the sessions. Perhaps they feel jealous that we have other clients, and they become angry or more emotionally charged, trying to pull back some of the power. We might provide too much advice or scaffolding to the individual, and they feel constricted by the work, ultimately feeling helpless (powerless). We might bring our cultural biases to the work, giving the individual only one side of the viewpoints instead of encouraging reflection and finding answers that feel right to them. As the individual may not trust their own judgment, we might collude with this by expecting them to only listen to our opinions. Alternatively, the individual may feel they do not need support and reject everything we offer, causing the practitioner to withdraw or lock antlers, creating more friction. The multitude of seemingly simple examples here came to me quickly, highlighting the need for a different way of thinking for the practitioner, so that we do not get tied up in the repeating of patterns of interpersonal relationships that the individual has always known. Using the model of ICAT, we can begin to think about the function of the behaviours in an attachment theory framework and start to address the interpersonal constructs that the individual—and we as practitioners—have created when working in power dynamics. Attachment theory tells us that if the relationship does not feel right and is not achieving its aim, there is a feeling of insecurity in the room. If an individual completely relies on us and we lean into that, are they afraid to take control of their lives, and are we afraid of letting go of that control? If we extend this deeper into interpersonal constructs, has the individual never had an experience of being in control because their mother, for example, never trusted them? Are we always in control because we never trusted our father, for example, to keep us in mind and look after us? Both parties hold the dichotomous construct of trust/mistrust, giving us information on their attachment needs in the relationship. Therefore, with our knowledge of a lack of safety and both the individual and therapist reacting to a lack of trust, the focus of the work through ICAT becomes how the practitioner can trust the individual to bring positive change into their lives. Not only does this focus address the interpersonal and attachment needs in the relationship, but it also provides a new way of being in a more equitable, and collaborative, power dynamic for both the individual and the practitioner.

Three Step Awareness: Attune, Mentalise, Act

To become aware of all of the elements of the interpersonal relationships we are in, professionally and personally, we have to notice. We need to move between being in the moment and almost hovering above it so that we can observe what is happening. One of the most tried and tested metaphors that I use with students and supervisees is that of keeping one foot on the riverbank, whilst the other is in the river. By this, I mean that to be able to truly help someone in any aspect of life, we need to be able to feel what is happening and, at the same time, remain objective so that we can think clearly about all of the options available. If we are fully in the water with the individual, we will become overwhelmed with their experiences, often being triggered by any echoes of similar experiences in our own world (projection and projective identification—thank you, Melanie Klein, 1946). If this happens, we, the practitioners, become unthinking and only react, whereas our job dictates that we need to think clearly about the individual's situation in order to provide a new way of being for the individual. Conversely, if we are completely on the riverbank, we are not feeling or thinking about the experience of the individual, and we are simply observing as an outsider. We cannot think from this standpoint either, as we are just looking and not feeling. So we need to be both, we need to be subjective and objective, inside and outside, feeling *and* thinking.

To hold the balance in the relationship and ensure that power is thought about and appropriate support is given, we need to hone our observation skills—through affect attunement (see Part I). We can notice physical things such as body language, where both individuals and practitioners are sitting in the room, etc. We can also notice emotional and attachment behaviours. This could be how it feels to be in the room with someone, what emotions we the practitioners are feeling and how our body feels, what happens when we put in a boundary or constraint, what happens when we offer advice and guidance. By closely observing the individual's reactions as well as our own, we can gather information that will help us support the work. Outside of therapeutic work, there is often an emphasis on the practitioner noticing the individual's reactions only and not their own. However, I really believe that we can be the barometers in this kind of interpersonal work, as our physical and emotional reactions tell us information as to what is being played out in the relationship. The feelings we react to in interpersonal work are very rarely about us; it is most often the individual's unconscious working out ways to get their needs for safety met; this is also known as transference and countertransference—one of the few remaining elements of Freud (1912).

There will be times when observing and noticing is enough—even in the focused work of TAF and MKO. The individual we are working with may not need advice at every utterance; I don't suppose anyone really does. At other times, the individual may have made a heavy disclosure or deep emotional connection between events and behaviours, and we need to have the confidence to let this feeling be. By not offering a fix or advice, we can acknowledge the depth of feeling in the room and simply feel. We may also notice some nonverbal information from the individual that they do not want us to speak or offer, but that they want us to hear. Again, with power comes responsibility, so we must use the ability to observe and notice carefully. Some individuals may need verbal or nonverbal reassurance, and we need to provide that in order to create that safety. To use our river metaphor, we don't want the individual to feel like we are standing on the riverbank in an unfeeling way. By developing our attunement skills, we react and support in a way that is meaningful to the individual in that moment. Attunement is the ability to feel and think at the same time; it is seeing and acknowledging the need in the other.

Once we have attuned to observe and acknowledge the need in the relationship, we can begin to act. The first step to acting is mentalisation. We have seen and felt the need in the individual, and now we mentalise the action we must take to meet the need. So, we move from observing the feelings in ourselves and the individual to thinking, "what does it feel like we need to do?" We will use our interpersonal constructs and our DRs to tell us some of this information, and we will use trial and error, modelling curiosity in a safe place. Let's use an example here. We have an angry student who is disrupting classes. We might have offered them a series of sessions where we have slowly built up trust, and there is calm, or the psychic Zone of Proximal Development. As we work on a task together in this safe space, perhaps something creative, we can attune to the feelings in the room. We can ask ourselves "What does it feel like now? Why would they get so angry?" Once we have noticed the feelings, we begin to mentalise and imagine a narrative for the feelings. By using the ICAT framework, we can shape those mentalisations—what is the function of the behaviours? What constructs have they created around school, teachers, learning, being with peers…? We might think that the student is acting out in class because they are finding the work too hard, and even though they have told the teacher this, no support has been added. Perhaps the student is acting out in school because they have punitive parents at home, and this is the only place they can be heard. In the safety of the relationship we have created, we can ask the individual about our mentalisations, opening a dialogue of possibilities which they can confirm or deny, adding their own thoughts and feelings collaboratively.

After attunement and mentalisation within the framework of ICAT, and in the role of the TAF/MKO, we need to think about action. ICAT itself is not concerned with outcomes (see the next chapter), but the specific roles we are discussing are concerned with outcomes. Those moments where we have built safety in the relationship have given us plenty of information to provide a plan for the individual to create positive change. In fact, by being attuned and imagining their internal experiences, we have already fostered a place of change in the constructs and DRs that the individual has previously stored on attachment and power figures. The course of action we offer needs to be co-created, especially as we are reflecting on power. I have found that Crittenden's guidance in Raising Parents (2015) is very helpful for practitioners when thinking about ways to practically support our clients, staff and students. I find that as practitioners, we will offer support related to our specific areas of knowledge, such as therapy or education, and this is right and just. Sometimes, however, we have an opportunity to think outside of our knowledge (perhaps seeking our own MKO) to meet the needs of the individual. This could be suggesting a therapy client with ADHD employs a cleaner to help with overwhelm in the home, thus giving them more space to think about other things. We could suggest that the student struggling with anger seeks the support of a therapist in order to help with engagement in the curriculum at school. Whatever we recommend must be based on the information we have collected from trying to understand the function of the behaviours presented, by providing a base of safety and a new way of interacting and with the best interests of the individual at heart.

Contexts for the Application of ICAT

The Interpersonal Constructs and Attachment Theory (ICAT) framework is not confined to a single professional domain. Rather, it offers a transdisciplinary lens for understanding how people anticipate, interpret, and respond to relational experience across a range of contexts. Because ICAT is concerned with safety, meaning-making, affect regulation, and relational flexibility, it is applicable wherever human relationships shape learning, wellbeing, and performance. This section outlines three primary contexts in which ICAT can be meaningfully applied: therapeutic practice, educational settings, and workplace environments.

Importantly, ICAT is not presented as a set of techniques to be imposed uniformly across contexts. Instead, it provides a relational stance and conceptual map that supports practitioners in responding thoughtfully to the conditions, capacities, and constraints of each environment. Across all contexts, the central question remains consistent: *what does this relational system need in order to support safety, reflection, and adaptive change?*

ICAT in Therapeutic Contexts

In therapeutic settings, ICAT offers a coherent framework for understanding emotional distress, relational difficulties, and patterns of behaviour as adaptive responses shaped by prior relational experience and current context. Clients enter therapy with established attachment strategies and interpersonal constructs that organise how they perceive the therapist, anticipate responses, and regulate emotion within the therapeutic relationship. From an ICAT perspective, these patterns are not obstacles to treatment but valuable sources of information about how the client has learned to remain safe in relationships.

Therapeutic work informed by ICAT prioritises the creation of a reliable holding environment in which affect attunement, mentalisation, and reflective dialogue can gradually emerge. The therapist functions as a transitional attachment figure and a more knowledgeable other, not by directing change, but by participating in a relational process that supports curiosity, flexibility, and the possibility of reconstruing meaning. Techniques such as noticing relational shifts, naming affect, exploring constructs without premature challenge, and repairing ruptures are grounded in this stance.

Crucially, ICAT also guides therapists in recognising when insight-oriented work is not yet appropriate. In contexts of ongoing danger, trauma, or neurobiological constraint, the therapeutic task may shift toward stabilisation, predictability, and regulation rather than interpretation. In this way, ICAT supports ethical practice by aligning intervention with relational readiness.

ICAT in Educational Contexts

In educational settings, ICAT provides a powerful framework for understanding learning as a relational and emotional process, rather than a purely cognitive one. Students bring attachment histories and interpersonal constructs into classrooms, shaping how they perceive authority, manage uncertainty, respond to feedback, and engage with peers. Behaviour that is often labelled as disengaged, oppositional, or unmotivated can be reinterpreted through ICAT as a strategy for managing perceived threat, shame, or unpredictability.

Educators using an ICAT-informed approach attend not only to curriculum and instruction, but also to relational consistency, emotional attunement, and the creation of psychologically safe learning environments. Predictable routines, clear boundaries, and responsive relationships function as holding structures that enable students to take risks, tolerate not knowing, and engage in reflective learning. Teachers and support staff act as relational anchors who can scaffold both academic and emotional development through attuned interaction and thoughtful repair following relational ruptures.

ICAT is particularly relevant in inclusive education, where neurodiversity, cultural difference, and varying attachment experiences require flexible, context-sensitive responses. Rather than assuming a single model of engagement or motivation, ICAT supports educators in adapting their relational approach to the individual student while maintaining coherence within the wider system.

ICAT in Workplace and Organisational Contexts

Within workplace and organisational settings, ICAT offers a lens for understanding patterns of communication, leadership, conflict, and performance as relationally organised phenomena. Employees and leaders alike bring attachment strategies and interpersonal constructs into professional roles, influencing how they experience authority, collaboration, feedback, and change. Organisational cultures themselves can be understood as systems of shared constructs that shape expectations about safety, productivity, and belonging.

An ICAT-informed approach to leadership and organisational practice emphasises the importance of relational predictability, psychological safety, and reflective capacity. Managers and leaders function as attachment-relevant figures, particularly during periods of uncertainty, restructuring, or stress. Attuned leadership—characterised by clear communication, consistent boundaries, and openness to dialogue—supports trust and engagement, while unacknowledged relational ruptures can activate defensive strategies that undermine co-operation and wellbeing.

ICAT also provides a framework for understanding resistance to change not as opposition, but as an adaptive response to perceived relational threat. By attending to the emotional and meaning-making dimensions of organisational life, practitioners can support teams and individuals to move from rigid, self-protective patterns toward more flexible and collaborative ways of working.

A Unifying Relational Framework

Across therapeutic, educational, and workplace contexts, ICAT functions as a unifying framework that foregrounds relationship as the medium through which change occurs. While the specific goals and boundaries of each context differ, the underlying processes of attachment, construct formation, affect regulation, and mentalisation remain consistent. By attending to these processes, practitioners are better equipped to respond ethically and effectively to complexity, difference, and distress.

The chapters that follow will explore how ICAT can be operationalised within these contexts, offering practical techniques, case material, and guidance on pacing and adaptation. In doing so, the aim is not to prescribe a single way of working, but to support practitioners in developing relational sensitivity, reflective flexibility, and confidence in navigating the interpersonal dimensions of their work.

Chapter 8
From Safety to Meaning: Integrating Attachment, Constructs, and the Relational Present

In the previous chapters, attachment theory and constructivist traditions have been explored as parallel yet deeply compatible ways of understanding how people develop, regulate emotion, and make sense of their relational worlds. This chapter brings those strands together in practice. It focuses on what must be present between people for thinking, flexibility, and change to become possible.

Rather than offering a sequence of techniques or a manualised intervention, this chapter introduces ICAT as a relational practice grounded in safety, predictability, and containment. From this foundation, attention turns to the relational here and now—the moment-to-moment interactions in which attachment strategies and interpersonal constructs are actively enacted. It is within these lived exchanges that anticipation, affect, and meaning intersect, and where opportunities for change most clearly arise.

The chapter argues that behaviour is best understood not as pathology to be corrected, but as information about safety, adaptation, and relational history. By shifting away from deficit-based interpretations and towards a functional understanding of behaviour, practitioners can reduce shame and support the development of more flexible, integrated ways of relating. The ICAT techniques presented here are therefore not prescriptive steps, but relational capacities that become available once sufficient safety has been established. Their ethical and effective use depends on timing, context, and professional judgement.

Through theory, practice examples, and brief vignettes, this chapter aims to support practitioners across therapeutic, educational, and social care contexts to work with complexity without losing relational depth. In doing so, it seeks to demonstrate how attachment processes and interpersonal meaning-making can be integrated into a coherent, humane, and practical framework for change.

Within ICAT, practitioners are guided less by prescriptive technique and more by a consistent orienting question: What does this relational system need right now to make thinking possible? This question holds together attachment, interpersonal constructs, and mentalisation, ensuring that intervention follows safety rather than

R. Swanick, *A Clinical Guide to Interpersonal Constructs and Attachment Theory*, https://doi.org/10.1007/978-3-032-23728-6_8

precedes it. At each point when interacting with another as the practitioner, we need to remember that behaviour is a function of safety and gives us information. If we look beyond the presenting behaviour to the feelings underneath, we will be able to see and then meet the needs of that individual. By moving away from behaviour as a pathology, as in something that is treated in a medical model, and towards behaviour as a function or information, we take away the "right and wrong" and any associated shame for individuals. This is one of the first steps in creating safety: practitioners can acknowledge that the presenting behaviour was adaptive in an unsafe context and now it does not serve the individual well in the present context.

ICAT is not a discrete intervention designed to produce change; it is a relational practice that supports safety, reflection, and flexibility in "good enough" contexts. The techniques outlined below are therefore offered as orienting practices rather than prescriptive steps, and their ethical use depends on timing, context, and relational readiness. We are beginning to fully transform our theory into practice.

Relational Preconditions

Before any relational technique can be effective in any context, be that therapy, educational or work-based, certain preconditions must be present. Within ICAT, these preconditions are understood as foundational rather than optional. Providing a sense of safety, predictability and containment for individuals will support positive change in their interpersonal constructs and dispositional representations. Without these stabilisers in the relationship, it may not be possible for adaptive change to happen.

Safety

Safety refers to the individual's subjective sense that the relational space is not threatening. Feeling safe is beyond the absence of a physical threat. Over my many years working in trauma, I have seen clients become triggered and upset in the safest spaces you can imagine. To understand why this may happen, we can return to ethology (see Part One). Early humans and animals were/are wired for safety. Their whole nervous systems were set up to detect the smallest threat, as any type of injury could result in death, and the possible end of their genetic line. Crittenden often talks about attachment relationships being for safety *and* reproduction—and sure, babies are very lovely, but essentially we are reproducing so we can ensure the continuation of our family line and the human race on a very genetic level. We have noticed in this book how the maternal brain physically changes so that the infant is protected. This is love and nurture, but it is also essential in keeping the human race alive. These instincts of protection and seeking safety are not exclusive to early humans or our contemporary evolutionary stage: they are phylogenetic, meaning that they genetically inherited innate drives that have been naturally selected over millions of years to ensure survival (Gilbert, 2024). When the brain is triggered to feel unsafe, through a physical, emotional, or interpersonal event, humans will react in a fight, flight, or freeze way. We all have a default setting or a certain reaction which we will use most, as in line with our DRs and constructs, but we will use all of these behaviours at points in our lives.

- Fight—This is when our body prepares to physically defend itself. We will notice this by a rise in anxiety, increased blood flow through the body, clenched muscles, particularly around the shoulders and jaw, and even clenched fists.
- Flight—This is when your body is preparing to escape. Again, anxious feelings increase, and you start to feel restless, trapped and fidgety. Your breathing may increase, and you will experience a very real feeling to run or flee.
- Freeze—This is what happens when your brain does not know what to do. It shuts down. You will be numb, dissociated, perhaps like you are watching the situation from above. You might feel emotionally stuck as your body is "playing dead".

The behaviours described here can be linked to our attachment strategies. Type A strategies, those who omit the negative affects and present in an over independent or coping way, will often use flight as their technique. As the levels of threat rise, Type A will become overwhelmed by the amount of negative emotional information they are processing and as their natural state is not to express those negative feelings, they will want to leave the situation. Type C strategies, those who distort information so that they can survive, will oscillate between fight and flight. In the Dynamic Maturational Model (DMM, described in Part One), the definitions of the types of attachment strategies reflect this—we have the person who feigns helplessness then becomes aggressive, or the seducer and punisher. Type C has learned that using one type of behaviour will not get them the attention they need, and so they have to employ a range to ensure their caregiver (or whoever it is in their DRs) maintains that attention. Freeze can happen in any situation, especially if we are finding it hard to process the threatening information. However, it is most present in Type A+C+, or the traditionally classified Disorganised, strategies. Individuals usually present with this range of strategies (as that is what Type A+C+ is by definition) because they (or their caregiver) have enduring mental health challenges and/or their caregiver is represented internally as someone to fear, whilst also instigating a feeling of needing safety from them. These DRs mean that when the individual experiences a threat, they completely dissociate, which can look like someone who is very spaced-out and disconnected, or someone in a state of huge emotional turmoil. As I shared in Part One, this level of distress was not often seen in my work with families experiencing trauma. When I did see young people or parents in a state of dissociation or mental collapse, it was frightening and upsetting for everyone. This type of presentation is seen most in times of ongoing conflict, and in the reasons people are incarcerated or in secure medical facilities.

In order to understand our physiological responses to threat and safety, we will now explore Bruce Perry's Hierarchy of Brain Development (2006). When adults react to perceived threat or to feeling unsafe, their behaviours may return to an earlier stage of development as their default reactions are triggered. Having this information from Perry will help you as practitioners to fine tune your observation skills and support you in your mentalisations when working with individuals. When adults, or older children, "act out" in a way to show their distress, it can be because they have unresolved feelings from an earlier time in their lives, and now, they are behaving in a way that they know guarantees attention for their needs to be met. There is a saying, "a leopard can't change its spots", which fits here. However, my argument through this book, and in all my work, is that we *can* change our spots if we have the right attachment figures around us. So let us continue by exploring the theory of Bruce Perry.

Perry's Hierarchy is part of his model of Neurodevelopment (2006), and he states that the brain processes information developmentally in a "bottom-upwards" way (see Fig. 8.1).

The figure above shows that the brainstem is the first area to develop, and it is the only fully working part of the brain available to us at birth. The brainstem is responsible for our fight, fight or freeze reactions, and this really emphasises the importance of those first early attachment experiences in how we will go on to manage stress in the future. Physiologically, the brainstem controls our heart rate, body temperature and blood pressure. When the brainstem is regulated, so are we. When the brainstem feels threatened, our heart rate, blood pressure, and body temperature are

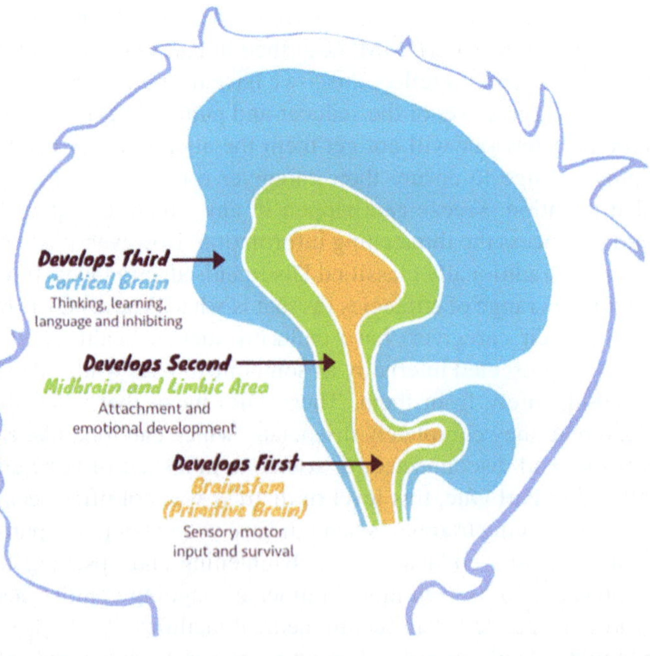

Fig. 8.1 Bruce Perry's hierarchy of brain development, from Beacon House Resources (2019)

altered, and that is how we know we are experiencing stress or threat. In good enough contexts, the caregiver will nurture their infant during brainstem development, providing Winnicott's ideas of holding to help the infant to be and to feel regulated and secure in those important first 8 months of life. If the caregiver cannot do this, for many reasons, the infant will not learn how to self-regulate, and there will be holes in their emotional development. Just as when we plant a seed in the garden, it will find a way to grow, the brain does not stop developing even if the conditions around it are not good enough. Therefore, in Perry's Hierarchy, the brain will continue to develop even if all of the milestones for security were not reached in the initial brainstem stage.

The next stage of development is the midbrain and limbic system, which grows from birth to when the infant is around 4 years old. This is the time we cement our attachment and regulation systems, learning who we can trust, who we like to be around, and how to begin to manage those big feelings we experience. At this point in life, we need an attachment figure who is going to keep us physically safe as we begin to explore the outside world through play and movement. We also need someone who can help us to understand our feelings, as the preoperational brain growth that happens here means that everything can feel more intense; do you recognise your toddler or the 3-year-old you worked with here?. If all goes well at this stage, we have children who know they can rely on their caregivers to consistently keep them physically and emotionally safe. We can literally sleep soundly at night knowing that someone is looking after us. When things are more challenging within this period, children find it hard to regulate their emotions and more pronounced attachment strategies come into action. In our practitioner clinics or schools, we might see a reserved and shy child who doesn't like leaving their parent or talking to others, or we see the beginnings of Type C strategies in the child who finds it hard to sit still and engage. According to Perry, the first 5 years of human life dictate 90% of brain development, and this will create the blueprint of our reactions and regulation into adult life.

The final stage of Perry's Hierarchy is in the cortical brain. This happens from 5 to 25 years and is the development into concrete and abstract thought, it is where we learn how to mentalise and think for ourselves, and it is where we learn social constructs and inhibition. (Mousley et al. (2025) *have found that brains do keep developing until the age of 32, which extends Perry's findings.*) Executive functioning is a key skill in these early years of more independence—and as contemporary research grows, I think this will be an important area in the near future. Executive functioning develops in the prefrontal cortex of the brain, and it is how the brain organises information so we can organise our lives physically and emotionally. Our working memory, the ability to write a number down whilst listening to another, for instance, our inhibitory control, that is our ability to resist distractions and remain focused on a task, and our cognitive flexibility, how we can adjust our thinking to new information and plans, are all held within the executive function of the brain. In Perry's Hierarchy, this area is the last to develop, and it is a conscious process; we do not have an innate ability to organise ourselves in a functioning way. We have to learn through good enough contexts and relationships, co-regulation and those important "Others" such as the Resilient, the Transitional Attachment and the More Knowledgeable. There are outliers to the growth of executive functioning, such as neurodivergence, and we will come to this in later chapters. Executive functioning is an interpersonally learned set of skills that we need to function as prosocial humans in adult life.

If everything has developed in a good enough way, and the individual has some executive functioning skills available to them, then in times of threat, they can rely on those past experiences and DRs to support them to make positive decisions in how to manage feelings of insecurity. If, however, the individual did not have those early regulatory needs met, and has internalised a maladaptive set of DRs, then their decisions will be defaulted to the brainstem, resulting in fight, flight or freeze reactions. As stated several times in this book, we are what we repeatedly do, and with our brain looking for efficiencies of energy at every point, we will default to our trusted behaviours when we feel fearful.

Predictability

Another way to think about default behaviours and brain efficiencies is predictability. When we are in dialogue with another person, safe or unsafe, we are using our interpersonal constructs to seek signals so that we can predict the behaviour of another person. When we can predict how someone else will react in a situation, the body feels safe as it "knows" what to do next. This is true even when the predicted reaction is dangerous. When an environment is consistent, such as the use of routines and the same caregivers, the brain uses much less energy through hypervigilant scanning for threats and can devote more energy to executive functioning, making it easier for the individual to live their life. This remains the case—and I am going to keep repeating this—even when the environment is not safe to an onlooker. It is important to note this, especially if we are working in child protection services, as it can explain the behaviours of the child both within and outside of the "dangerous" context. If, for example, a child grows up in a calm house, where their parents attend to their every need and all is well, then we move them to a chaotic school environment where there is noise and many personalities, we can understand how the child will feel dysregulated in the school environment, as we *know* how this would feel unsafe. If the child is at home and there is aggression and violence, and their parent rarely offers attention, whilst in school, the teacher is nurturing and the classroom calm, the child becomes dysregulated in the school environment for the same reason as our first example here. The child cannot predict what could potentially happen in environments which are contrary to their home environments. The environment which has the most meaning and connection for the child will become their safe place, whether that is deemed safe or not by practitioners. The internal message is "I know what is going to happen here so I can keep myself safe". When there is perceived chaos—an intense way of being that is different to the individual's norm—then the brain has to use a lot of energy to survive, and rational decisions become difficult.

Being predictable for someone else means you are being consistent and, in our frame of ICAT, appropriately responsive. It is not about rigidity, as that often serves the needs of one but not the other; it is about being flexible. I am always aware of how conscious you have to be of someone's needs in order for your responses to be consistent, especially in a work or parenting context. Predictability and consistency are all of those traits we have talked about in attachment theory—it is the mother who responds in an attuned way to the infant crying, it is the caregiver who knows that Wednesdays are football days and they can't work late, it is the teacher who knows that the class needs to time to settle and offers a starter activity, it is the manager who turns up every week for the staff meeting. Predictability and consistency can even be found in strangers and in the environment where we live. I really struggle with the dark and damp months of the new year here in the UK, and I know that when I see the buds growing on the magnolia tree in my garden, warmer, brighter days are coming, and I won't always feel like this. These behavioural traits lead to resilience—we can trust others, that we will survive this difficult time, that Spring will follow Winter—and this all leads to better life satisfaction and those really important prosocial behaviours.

To help the brain and body feel safe, as practitioners, we can offer the same time for our meetings and sessions to individuals on the same day. The brain recognises this and thinks, Monday equals Music Therapy Day and once the individual gets used to the routine, their nervous system relaxes and they feel safe. We can also be consistent in our responses—I find this the most important in my work with children, adults, families, students, therapists and as a parent. This comes through attunement and being open with individuals, and your own sense of safety as a practitioner. For example, when you are working with an individual who uses Type A strategies, they may expect the practitioner to "tell them off" when they share something. By consistently responding in a calm way and acknowledging the positive experience of sharing feelings, the individual can reset their DRs through the predictability of the practitioner. This method, interestingly, has a similar effect on Type C, even though the strategies being used are varied. The consistent responses offered by the practitioner to the presenting behaviours in Type C bring that oscillating feeling towards balance. In parenting, we see this, and in management, too… and in every interpersonal relationship. If safety is the destination, then predictability —and our next element—will be how we get there.

Emotional Containment

When I think of emotional containment, I always get a visual image in my mind of someone putting all of their feelings into the little drawers of an apothecary cabinet and closing them back up. At any time, the drawers can come open, releasing the feelings, and we can choose to close them ourselves (when we feel regulated), and sometimes we need someone to close them for us (when we feel dysregulated). The cabinet is always there, with all of the feelings; it is just that sometimes we feel certain ones more as the drawers are opened.

Wilfred Bion (1897–1979) was the first to write about containment in a therapeutic and familiar sense (1962). In his psychoanalytic observations, he noted that the mother would "absorb" the feelings of the infant, internally make sense of them and then give them back to the infant with a name or gesture that felt appropriate for the infant to understand. Containment, therefore, needs to affect attunement first: the mother needs to sense what the infant is feeling in order to *make sense* of the feeling. The aim of containment is to regulate the infant's emotions so that they don't feel overwhelmed by them. This is called co-regulation. It is incredibly important in all interpersonal relationships—not just in infancy. If we know that when we feel overwhelmed, the other person can cope and help us to think about our feelings, we begin to trust them. *We feel safe with them.* As we noted in Part One, when we discussed the different types of attachment strategies, if there isn't a safe emotional space for us, we develop adaptive coping techniques where we either omit negative information (Type A) or we distort the information (Type C) in order to regulate ourselves. If we have had good enough care in early life, and this remains so as we develop through life, we can trust ourselves to feel those big emotions because we have internalised security in ourselves through our relationships with others; we move from dysregulated to regulated and from being contained to self-containment. *That is not to say we only have to self-contain when we get to adulthood. We need people around us whom we can rely on at all times in our lives.*

For containment to work well enough, we need to be predictable and consistent. When someone is sharing a big feeling with us, we can hold space that feels safe by not judging or rejecting the individual. This can be harder than it sounds—our own interpersonal constructs get in the way sometimes, and we react based on those rather than what the individual needs at that moment. For example, if the practitioner is a person who finds it hard to let go and cry, and their client or student starts to cry, the practitioner might subconsciously judge them for being……[you fill in the blanks here—vulnerable, a baby, weak, too much, etc.]. As professionals, we need to be very aware of our biases so that we do not project those onto the people we work with. This leads us on to the next requirement for containment—we need to be present rather than perfect. When someone is feeling overwhelmed, it can trigger us too, and we may end up in the river with them. By really being present, by really listening and feeling and thinking (thinking is the key here), we can contain their feelings and help them to manage them in a way that is useful in that moment. If we aim for perfection, then we may miss a cue or put our own feelings first, or become swept along in the river, and this isn't helpful for anyone. Another therapeutic term we could use here is *boundaries*. Boundaries are emotional and physical stances that keep us safe on the riverbank when we are dealing with difficult feelings in interpersonal relationships. Boundaries help us to acknowledge our own feelings and those that belong to someone else. They help us to know what we can help with and what needs to go to a different person or service. They are also another way of thinking of the physical constraints of working with people—the time we give, the venue, the intervention and the equipment available to our clients, students, and staff. Boundaries are there so we as professionals do not get overwhelmed with other people's feelings, and so we can remain the thinking person in the network around us.

If we don't have boundaries, containment, and predictability, then we cannot feel safe. This leads to adaptive attachment strategies that cause the individual to use whatever they can to feel safe. It means that individuals become dysregulated and feel out of control, experiencing anxiety, depression and other mental ill-health conditions. Without these preconditions, then therapeutic, educational or managerial interventions will not be successful. Most importantly, these are not techniques we might try; they are prerequisites for safe and trusting relationships in any context where people are functioning in interpersonal relationships.

Using the Here and Now

In ICAT-informed practice, meaningful change does not arise from the application of techniques in response to pre-defined formulations. Instead, it emerges through careful attention to what is unfolding in the relational *here and now*. The present moment is where attachment strategies are enacted, meanings are tested, and emotional regulation is either supported or threatened. It is therefore the primary site of assessment, intervention, and learning.

The "here and now" refers not simply to chronological immediacy, but to the *relational field* created between people in interaction. It is a term created by Irvin Yalom (b. 1931), and he writes about it beautifully in many of his books, most specifically in The Gift of Therapy (2009).

This book is truly one of my all-time favourites and I love dipping into it for advice, to be reminded of what I do and why I do it, and also to be reminded of my humanness in all of this. In fact, Yalom's book 'Love's Executioner' was one of the reasons I decided to be a therapist, so go read them all. I have digressed again...

When thinking of the here and now, tone of voice, pacing, bodily orientation, emotional shifts, moments of hesitation or intensity, and subtle changes in engagement all provide live information about safety, anticipation, and meaning-making. In ICAT, these moment-to-moment processes are treated as more informative than retrospective accounts alone, as they reveal how dispositional constructs and attachment strategies operate in real time.

Attention to the here and now is only possible when sufficient safety, predictability, and containment have been established. Where threat remains high, individuals are likely to rely on familiar self-protective strategies that limit reflection and flexibility. As containment strengthens, however, these strategies begin to appear *within* the relationship itself, offering practitioners the opportunity to notice, understand, and respond to them as they occur rather than interpreting them at a distance.

Working in the present moment allows practitioners to observe how expectations shape perception and behaviour. Anticipations about rejection, abandonment, control, or failure often become visible through shifts in affect, changes in rhythm, or sudden relational ruptures. These manifestations are not viewed as resistance or pathology within ICAT, but as meaningful adaptations to perceived relational risk. By staying with the here and now, practitioners can respond to these adaptations as they arise, supporting regulation and understanding before attempting exploration or change.

Importantly, a focus on the here and now does not exclude attention to history, context, or narrative. Rather, it situates past experience and future expectation within lived interaction. When an individual reacts strongly to a seemingly minor relational event, the present moment becomes a bridge between past attachment experiences and current meaning-making. The practitioner's task is not to interpret this connection prematurely, but to remain present with the experience as it unfolds, allowing meaning to emerge collaboratively.

The here and now also includes the practitioner's own internal experience. Feelings of urgency, uncertainty, reassurance-seeking, frustration, or withdrawal may signal aspects of the relational field that are difficult for the other person to hold alone. In ICAT, such responses are treated as potential sources of information rather than errors to be eliminated, provided that they are reflected upon and ethically managed. Attention to one's own anticipations and emotional shifts supports more attuned and responsible relational engagement.

By grounding practice in the here and now, ICAT resists both over-intellectualisation and premature intervention. It encourages practitioners to privilege presence over progress, curiosity over certainty, and responsiveness over technique. From this stance, relational moves such as attunement, marked mirroring, construct exploration, or repair become available not as steps to be followed, but as context-sensitive responses to what the relationship is asking for in that moment.

In this way, the here and now functions as the orienting lens through which ICAT techniques are selected, timed, and adapted. It is the point at which attachment processes, construct systems, and relational ethics converge, shaping how safety is maintained, meaning is explored, and change becomes possible.

Key ICAT Techniques—Relational Capacities Rather Than Sequential Interventions

The ICAT framework does not propose a staged or linear model of intervention. Instead, it identifies a set of relational techniques that become available to practitioners once sufficient safety, containment, and connection have been established. These techniques are not applied in a fixed order, nor are they all required in every interaction. Rather, they function as relational moves that may be drawn upon responsively, depending on the individual, relational, and contextual conditions present at any given moment.

From an ICAT perspective, technique is inseparable from the relationship. Each technique both reflects and reshapes the attachment–construct cycle in which the practitioner and client are jointly embedded. The following techniques therefore operate simultaneously at emotional, cognitive, and relational levels.

Attunement (Affect, Rhythm, and Vitality)

Attunement forms the foundation of all ICAT-informed work. It involves the practitioner's capacity to sense, resonate with, and respond to the emotional and relational state of the other, not only in terms of explicit affect, but also rhythm, intensity, and vitality.

This includes:

- Sensitivity to emotional tone (e.g. anxiety, withdrawal, excitement)
- Awareness of pacing (speed of speech, pauses, escalation or slowing)
- Responsiveness to non-verbal cues such as posture, gaze, and energy

In ICAT, attunement is not merely empathic understanding; it is a regulatory process through which emotional safety is co-created. Attuned responses help stabilise arousal, reduce perceived threat, and signal relational availability. Importantly, attunement is dynamic rather than static. Practitioners continually adjust their responses as emotional states shift, recognising that misattunement is inevitable and reparable.

Attunement creates the conditions under which other ICAT techniques become possible. Without it, interventions risk being experienced as intrusive, invalidating, or unsafe.

Marked Mirroring

Marked mirroring refers to the practitioner's capacity to reflect emotional states back to the client in a way that is recognisable yet clearly differentiated. The practitioner mirrors the affect, but does so *markedly*—signalling that the emotion is understood without being overwhelmed by it or mistaking it for their own.

In ICAT practice, marked mirroring serves several functions:

- It helps individuals recognise and name internal states
- It supports emotional integration rather than escalation
- It differentiates self from others, strengthening boundaries

For example, reflecting distress with a softened tone and explicit markers such as "It seems as though…" or "I wonder if…" allows the client to feel seen without feeling absorbed or replicated. This is particularly important for individuals with histories of emotional misattunement, intrusion, or neglect, where unmarked mirroring may feel either overwhelming or absent.

Marked mirroring supports the development of emotional coherence and lays the groundwork for reflective functioning, but it does not require immediate insight or verbal elaboration. Its primary function is containment and recognition, not interpretation.

Mentalising Dialogue

Mentalising dialogue involves conversational practices that promote curiosity about internal states—one's own and those of others—while explicitly holding uncertainty. In ICAT, mentalisation is treated as a *capacity that fluctuates*, rather than a stable trait.

Mentalising dialogue is characterised by:

- Tentative language ("I wonder…", "Could it be that…?")
- Multiple perspectives being held simultaneously
- Curiosity rather than certainty
- Sensitivity to emotional arousal

Importantly, ICAT does not assume that mentalisation is always appropriate or available. In moments of high affect or perceived threat, attempts to mentalise may feel invalidating or overwhelming. At such times, practitioners may prioritise attunement or mirroring, returning to reflective dialogue only when regulation allows.

Mentalising dialogue also applies to the practitioner's own experience. ICAT encourages explicit awareness of how professional responses are shaped by the relational field, including emotional reactions, assumptions, and anticipations.

Construct Exploration (Without Challenge)

A distinctive feature of ICAT is its emphasis on exploring meaning without premature challenge. Construct exploration involves gently bringing attention to how individuals organise experience—their assumptions, expectations, and interpretive frameworks—without immediately attempting to correct, reframe, or dispute them.

This includes exploration of:

- Core and peripheral constructs
- Implicit binaries (e.g. safe/dangerous, worthy/unworthy)
- Anticipatory meanings ("What did you expect would happen?")
- Relational rules and narratives

In ICAT, constructs are understood as adaptive, historically situated, and protective. Challenging them too early risks destabilising the very strategies that have enabled psychological survival. Exploration, by contrast, communicates respect for the internal logic of the person's world.

Through sustained exploration, constructs often begin to loosen organically. Alternative meanings may emerge not because they are imposed, but because the individual becomes aware of the limits and costs of existing interpretations. Change arises through expanded meaning-making, not persuasion.

Repair After Rupture

Rupture is inevitable in any meaningful relational work. From an ICAT perspective, rupture is not a failure of practice but a central site of therapeutic potential. What matters is not the absence of rupture, but the presence of repair.

Repair after rupture involves:

- Recognising when attunement has been lost
- Naming the relational disruption
- Taking appropriate responsibility
- Re-establishing emotional connection

Repair is particularly significant for individuals whose attachment histories include unacknowledged harm, abandonment, or misattunement. Experiencing a relationship in which ruptures are noticed and addressed—rather than denied, blamed, or ignored—provides a powerful corrective relational experience.

In ICAT, repair also supports construct change. It challenges deeply held expectations, such as "conflict means rejection" or "If I express discomfort, I'll be punished." Repair, therefore, operates simultaneously at attachment, emotional, and meaning-making levels.

Trusting Your Instinct

Crucially, these techniques are not steps in a sequence. An ICAT-informed practitioner may move fluidly between attunement, mirroring, exploration, and repair—sometimes within a single interaction. At other times, only one of these may be appropriate.

What guides their use is not protocol, but relational judgement:

- What does this person need *right now?*
- What is the emotional temperature of the interaction?
- Which intervention will support safety without foreclosing growth?

By presenting ICAT techniques as a flexible repertoire rather than a prescribed pathway, the model remains responsive to complexity, diversity, and context. It honours the relational nature of change and resists the reduction of therapeutic work to technique alone.

Brief Case Vignettes

These examples are intentionally concise, focusing on moments of relational decision-making rather than full case formulations in adult therapy, child and family work, and educational or organisational settings. Their purpose is to demonstrate how ICAT principles guide practice moment by moment, rather than to model idealised outcomes.

Adult Therapy: Working in the Here-and-Now

During a mid-session pause, an adult client becomes noticeably quieter after the therapist glances briefly at the clock. The client crosses their arms and begins to speak more generally about work, moving away from the previously emotional topic.

Rather than redirecting the conversation or offering reassurance, the therapist slows the pace and notes, *"Something shifted just then. I wonder if that moment felt different for you"*. The client initially shrugs, then says, *"I thought you were bored"*.

Within an ICAT framework, the therapist does not challenge this interpretation but explores it as an interpersonal construct shaped by earlier relational experience. Through gentle mentalising dialogue, the therapist reflects that the client learned to monitor others closely for signs of withdrawal, and that this strategy once helped them stay emotionally safe. By naming the misattunement and clarifying intention, the therapist repairs the rupture in the moment, offering a live experience of relational flexibility rather than abandonment. The therapeutic focus remains on process rather than reassurance, allowing the client to revise anticipations within a safe relational context.

Child and Family Work: Attunement and Repair

A 6-year-old child repeatedly interrupts sessions by knocking over toys and moving rapidly between activities. The parent apologises frequently, appearing anxious and controlling.

Instead of addressing behaviour directly, the practitioner attunes to the child's high energy by matching pace and tone, joining the play briefly before slowing it down. The practitioner comments, *"It feels like your body has lots of fast energy today"*, rather than asking the child to calm down. The child pauses, then nods.

Later, the practitioner reflects with the parent on how the child's behaviour may function as a self-protective strategy in moments of uncertainty. Without blaming or instructing, the practitioner supports the parent in noticing their own anxiety and how it shapes their responses. A moment of misattunement occurs when the practitioner interrupts the child's play; this is acknowledged openly and repaired, modelling for both child and parent that mistakes can be named and mended. Within ICAT, the focus remains on co-regulation, shared meaning, and the gradual development of relational safety rather than behavioural compliance.

Educational or Workplace Context: Construct Exploration Without Challenge

A student repeatedly avoids group work, stating, *"People always judge me if I say the wrong thing"*. In supervision, a similar pattern emerges with a staff member who avoids meetings, describing them as "pointless and political".

Rather than reframing or disputing these beliefs, the educator explores the construct underlying the avoidance. Through curiosity, the practitioner invites reflection on where the expectation of judgement originated and how it once served a protective function. The educator acknowledges the reality of power dynamics while also creating predictability and emotional containment in the learning environment.

Over time, small moments of attuned interaction—being listened to without interruption, having contributions acknowledged—allow the student and staff member to test alternative relational experiences. Change occurs not through persuasion but through repeated micro-experiences that soften rigid anticipations and allow more flexible participation. In ICAT terms, attachment strategies and interpersonal constructs become open to revision through lived relational safety rather than instruction.

Cross-Context Reflection

Across these contexts, the practitioner's role is not to correct meaning but to hold a relational space in which meaning can be explored, felt, and revised. The practitioner is the facilitator. Each vignette illustrates how ICAT techniques operate at the level of micro-interaction: attunement precedes interpretation, rupture is acknowledged rather than avoided, and reflection emerges only when safety allows. The work remains grounded in the present relationship, where attachment strategies and interpersonal constructs are most alive and therefore most available for change.

Chapter 9
When Safety, Culture, or Neurobiology Shapes Relational Work

This chapter explores the ethical limits of relational meaning-making. While ICAT offers a powerful framework for understanding how attachment and interpersonal constructs shape experience, it does not assume that all contexts are ready for reflection or change. Safety, neurobiology, culture, and structural conditions profoundly influence what is possible within any relational system. In some circumstances, attempts to promote insight, curiosity, or narrative exploration may be premature or even harmful.

Rather than treating these situations as failures of engagement, this chapter understands them as meaningful indicators of context. By attending carefully to constraints—whether biological, cultural, traumatic, or structural—practitioners can adapt, slow, or temporarily set aside ICAT in service of ethical care. In doing so, ICAT remains a relational practice grounded not in technique, but in responsibility, humility, and respect for lived reality.

Why Context Matters

There are many familiar idioms in the English language that point to the importance of context. Phrases such as *"context is king"* or *"you can't judge a book by its cover"* remind us that what we see on the surface rarely tells the full story. In 2025, Batstra and Frances captured this succinctly when they argued that *"diagnosing the context is as important as diagnosing the individual"*. Within Interpersonal Constructs and Attachment Theory (ICAT), this idea is not a rhetorical position but an ethical necessity.

Context refers to the landscape in which a person's life is lived. It encompasses the personal, social, physical, and societal conditions that shape experience and expectation over time. These contextual influences contribute directly to the development of interpersonal constructs and dispositional representations (DRs),

R. Swanick, *A Clinical Guide to Interpersonal Constructs and Attachment Theory*, https://doi.org/10.1007/978-3-032-23728-6_9

influencing how individuals anticipate danger, seek safety, and interpret relationships. In ICAT, behaviour is therefore never understood in isolation from the context in which it has emerged.

Personal Context

Personal context includes genetic predispositions and health conditions, family histories of trauma, loss, or illness, and the expectations shaped by class, race, culture, education, religion, and family roles. It also includes individual characteristics such as temperament, gender and sexual identity, patterns of emotional expression, resilience, coping strategies, and motivation. These factors interact to shape how a person navigates relationships and responds to stress.

Social Context

Social context reflects the quality and availability of relational networks, including family, friends, colleagues, and community groups. It also includes social identity, moral codes, group norms, and expectations around behaviour—such as attitudes toward alcohol use, work, social media, or health. These shared meanings influence what is considered acceptable, risky, or valued within a given relational system.

Physical Context

Physical context refers to the environments in which individuals spend their time: homes, schools, workplaces, cultural spaces, and neighbourhoods. These environments carry implicit messages about safety, belonging, and predictability, and can either support or undermine regulation and relational engagement.

Societal Context

Societal context includes wider structural conditions such as housing, access to green space, urban or rural living, pollution, noise, infrastructure, educational systems, and work expectations. These factors shape opportunity, stress exposure, and long-term well-being, often in ways that are unevenly distributed across populations.

This list is not exhaustive. Contextual factors intersect—particularly through gender, race, class, health, and migration status—creating layered experiences of advantage or constraint. Research consistently shows that individuals born into socially privileged contexts tend to have greater access to education, employment, and psychological resources, while those experiencing marginalisation, displacement, chronic illness, or long-term trauma face significantly greater barriers. These disparities are not reflections of individual capacity, but of structural and relational conditions.

As explored throughout Parts One and Two, the brain is an efficient organ designed to prioritise survival. When individuals experience psychological or physical threat, the brain reduces access to reflective and integrative processes in favour of rapid protective responses. In such moments, the nervous system defaults to fight, flight, or freeze, and meaning-making gives way to survival. Anxiety, depression, and psychosomatic symptoms can be understood as expressions of this adaptive shift.

When distress arises from changes in context—such as unsafe relationships, poverty, discrimination, or instability—attempts to encourage reflection or insight may themselves become threatening. For adaptive change to occur, individuals must be supported not only internally, but relationally and contextually. This support often comes from Transitional Attachment Figures, More Knowledgeable Others, or Resilient Others. At times, however, the very people or systems that should provide safety are themselves sources of threat, leaving individuals without a secure base from which to reflect.

For practitioners, this raises a critical ethical question: not only *what* intervention is needed, but *when*. Timing is central to ICAT practice. Introducing insight or meaning-making too early risks increasing shame, dysregulation, or withdrawal. Delaying intervention too long may also cause harm by missing opportunities for stabilisation or change. In this sense, timing itself becomes a clinical intervention.

Before relational or reflective work can proceed, the preconditions outlined earlier in this book—safety, predictability, and containment—must be actively supported. In some cases, this means addressing practical or environmental factors before emotional work is possible. An individual may need to leave an unsafe relationship, change schools or workplaces, or access social care or alternative provision. Only once a key element of context has shifted can other factors—such as health needs, parenting capacity, or learning differences—be meaningfully explored.

This process often requires careful, incremental change. Altering one contextual variable at a time allows new boundaries to stabilise before further work is undertaken. For example, a child presenting with behaviours suggestive of autism may first require a change in educational environment. If regulation does not improve despite increased support, practitioners may then consider additional contextual factors such as sensory processing differences or routines at home. Each step provides new information, guiding further intervention without premature labelling or assumption.

Safety as the Precondition for Relational Work

While context shapes the conditions in which people live, safety determines what becomes possible within a relationship in the present moment. In ICAT-informed practice, safety is not understood as reassurance or the absence of conflict, but as a lived, embodied experience that allows the nervous system to remain regulated enough for attention, curiosity, and reflection to emerge. When safety is compromised, relational work does not simply become more difficult; it becomes qualitatively different. Attachment strategies intensify, interpersonal constructs narrow, and meaning-making gives way to survival. For this reason, safety is not an outcome of effective relational work, but it is a necessary starting point.

In this section, six lenses are proposed through which safety can be understood in professional practice. Each lens explores how safety and threat are experienced across bodies, relationships, meaning-making systems, and professional roles. The aim is to support practitioners to reflect deeply on how safety is compromised, how threat is communicated, and how these processes interact with the ICAT framework in both ourselves and others.

The Six Lenses of Safety

Safety as a Felt, Relational Experience

Lens: Embodied and interpersonal

Safety

When we feel safe, our bodies show it. Breathing is calm and regular, muscles are relaxed, and movement feels settled rather than restless. We can make appropriate eye contact, share affect, and engage in prosocial ways. We respond consistently, attend to verbal and non-verbal cues, and offer time and presence to others because our own needs feel sufficiently met. Safety does not need to be named; it is felt.

Threat

Under threat, the body tightens. Muscles tense, breathing becomes shallow, and physical symptoms such as headaches or stomach pain may emerge. Attention narrows, thinking becomes difficult, and we may become hypervigilant or dissociated. We struggle to read cues accurately, feel defensive, and experience a pervasive sense of dread or urgency. Words lose meaning, and non-verbal signals are easily misinterpreted.

ICAT Stance

Safety is communicated through relationship, not explanation. It is created through attunement, acknowledgement of distress, and co-regulation. Breathing together, consistent availability, and shared presence gradually allow the nervous system to settle. As regulation returns, muscles relax, eye contact increases, and affect can be shared.

A 10-year-old child returns home after masking distress all day at school. They avoid eye contact, pace the room, and refuse to speak. The parent stays nearby, acknowledges the child's feelings without pressure, and waits. The child gradually moves closer, eventually leaning into the parent's calm presence. Through quiet co-regulation, the child settles without needing to explain.

Safety as a Gatekeeper of Cognitive and Reflective Capacity

Lens: Neurobiological–functional

Safety

When safety is present, attention becomes available. We can be curious, playful, and reflective, experimenting with emotional and practical possibilities. We can mentalise our own needs, ask for help, and consider the perspectives of others. Problem-solving feels possible, and relationships feel manageable.

Threat

When safety is absent, the brain raises the drawbridge. Attention shifts from meaning to monitoring. Curiosity collapses, playfulness disappears, and thinking becomes rigid and catastrophic. High-level cognition gives way to brainstem-driven responses of fight, flight, or freeze.

ICAT Stance

Regulation precedes reflection. Basic physiological needs must be met before emotional or relational work can begin. Hunger, exhaustion, and exposure to danger further limit cognitive capacity. Once physical and relational safety are restored through trusted support, reflective thinking can gradually return.

A mother and child experiencing domestic abuse are referred to a practitioner. The practitioner prioritises practical safety: access to shelter, food, clothing, and rest. As their basic needs are met, trust develops. Only then does the mother begin to speak openly, allowing collaborative planning for longer-term safety.

Safety and the Activation of Attachment Strategies

Lens: Attachment-informed

Safety

When we feel secure, we trust others and can seek comfort when needed. Attachment strategies remain flexible and responsive to context. Problems are addressed collaboratively, with compromise and co-operation. Behaviour is steady, and relationships feel predictable.

Threat

When safety is uncertain, attachment strategies intensify. Trust collapses, help is either avoided or demanded urgently, and behaviour becomes polarised. Individuals may oscillate between withdrawal and aggression, independence and dependence. Everything feels overwhelming.

ICAT Stance

Strategies become louder when safety is uncertain. Behaviour is always communication. Sudden changes in behaviour signal that something is wrong, even when the behaviour appears maladaptive in a safe context. The practitioner's task is not to judge, but to understand and restore safety.

A high-performing staff member begins missing meetings and becomes aggressive when a routine change is announced. Through paced exploration, the manager learns that a sibling is critically ill. The perceived loss of connection at work reactivated fears of abandonment. Regular check-ins and consistent support restore a sense of security.

Safety and Interpersonal Construct Rigidity

Lens: Meaning-making and anticipation

Safety

When safe, we can accurately read cues, anticipate outcomes flexibly, and tolerate uncertainty. Constructs expand through interaction, and we can hold multiple emotions without becoming overwhelmed. Surprises are manageable.

Threat

Under threat, prediction becomes rigid. We default to familiar meanings, split experiences into good or bad, and act as though the present will replicate the past. Growth is sacrificed for perceived security.

ICAT Stance

When safety is low, meaning must protect rather than explore. Rigid constructs help individuals survive threats but limit adaptation in safer contexts. Flexible meaning-making becomes possible only when safety is restored.

A young person expects a new teacher to behave like a previous punitive one. Initial confrontational behaviour reflects this anticipation. With the support of a Transitional Attachment Figure, feelings and facts are explored separately, allowing the young person to revise expectations and engage more flexibly.

Safety as a Professional and Ethical Responsibility

Lens: Practitioner positioning

Safety

When practitioners feel supported, they show the same embodied signs of safety as any other individual—they are a human in the room, too. They use supervision, maintain boundaries, follow procedures, and feel able to repair mistakes. Reflection is possible.

Threat

Under professional threat, stress symptoms emerge, boundaries blur, and supervision is avoided. Practitioners may over-disclose, become rigid, or act defensively, inadvertently compromising client safety.

ICAT Stance

Safety is something practitioners help create, not something clients bring. Professional self-awareness, adherence to boundaries, and organisational support are essential to ethical relational work.

A therapist experiencing unprocessed bereavement attends a session with a client in crisis and over-discloses personal distress. The client withdraws and later complains. The investigation highlights the need for organisational responsibility and practitioner self-protection to maintain relational safety.

When Safety Is Not Yet Possible

Lens: Limits and restraints

In some situations, individuals are experiencing ongoing biological and relational threats. Severe trauma, illness, abuse, or neglect may leave the nervous system locked in survival mode. Reflection is not resisted; it is inaccessible.

ICAT Stance

Relational work must wait for safety, not force it. Ethical practice may involve holding space without interpretation, providing practical support, pausing therapy, or referring to alternative services. Practitioners must also recognise when their own responses are shaped by fear or avoidance.

To work fully and responsibly, practitioners must remain mindful of what they bring to the relational space. Safety is co-created. If one part of the system becomes unstable, the whole structure is compromised.

Across these six lenses, safety emerges as a dynamic, relational process rather than a fixed state. Whether viewed through the body, brain, attachment system, meaning-making, professional role, or ethical limits, the same principle applies: without safety, relational work cannot proceed as intended. ICAT, therefore, positions safety as a continual responsibility rather than a preliminary task. By attending carefully to how safety and threat are experienced moment by moment, practitioners can make informed decisions about pacing, timing, and intervention. Only when safety is sufficiently restored does reflection, flexibility, and relational change become possible—not because they are demanded, but because the nervous system is finally free to engage with the context around it.

Understanding safety as a relational and embodied process invites a further question: what happens when safety is shaped by fundamentally different neurobiological organisations, rather than by threat alone? Even in contexts where care is consistent and intentions are good, individuals may experience the world through nervous systems that process sensation, emotion, and relational information in markedly different ways. In such cases, difficulties in connection are not best understood as failures of attachment or deficits in regulation, but as mismatches between relational environments and neurodevelopmental needs. This next section explores how ICAT attends to neurobiological difference without pathologising it, and how relational work must adapt when safety, attunement, and meaning are organised differently from the assumed norm.

Differences in Relational Processing

The following section will describe and explore how certain development and contextual differences can affect interpersonal relationships, and how we create constructs and meaning in our lives. We will look at the effects of neurodiversity and trauma, as well as culture and power on our relationships—as not only will we see plenty of challenges around these issues in our professional work, it is also important to acknowledge our learning edges in relation to these elements. The differences described here are not exhaustive or even all-inclusive, as this would be a whole book itself. The aim is to provide some information on these differences that will affect relationships by exploring the challenges through the ICAT Stance. This will bring some understanding of how interpersonal and attachment constructs affect relationships in the here and now and help us as practitioners to reflect on that understanding. Remember, knowing who we are as practitioners will help keep us safe and create deeper safety for the individuals we work with, too.

Neurodiversity

Neurodiversity is an umbrella term used to describe variations in information processing in the brain. People who are neurodivergent will often learn and develop differently in comparison to what professionals would consider 'normal'. Individuals who are neurodivergent will also experience the world and relationships differently, meaning that social cues may not be read, there may be sensory challenges and also difficulties processing language, verbal or written information. Neurodiversity can include Dyslexia, Dyscalculia, Tourette's Syndrome, Attention Deficit Hyperactive Disorder (ADHD), and Autism Spectrum Condition (ASC). For the purposes of concentrating on interpersonal relationships, we will focus on ADHD and ASC.

Autism Spectrum Condition (ASC)

Autism in individuals is often characterised by differences in speech and language, in social relationships and needs, in interests and motivations and in physiological differences in brain development. A large study was conducted in 2011 by

Courchesne, Campbell, and Solso, which showed that in the first 4 years of life, the brains of individuals with autism grow more rapidly than in neurotypical development. The most prominent areas of growth are the frontal and temporal lobes, which are responsible for social cognition and language. However, by middle childhood, this development stops. As we have noted in Perry's hierarchical brain development model and in Crittenden's Dynamic Maturational Model, neither brains nor humans arrive on the planet fully formed. Our brains grow as we grow and are deeply affected by the context in which we are living. We can hypothesise that as the brain in individuals with autism stops or slows down early in human life, it will be hampered in processing the complex and nuanced social information that occurs in our interpersonal relationships. Another aspect of neurotypical brain development is that of neural pruning—we can come back to the Durant quote here, "*we are what we repeatedly do*". We know the brain likes to save energy, so when we get to adolescence, especially, the brain notices which communication pathways we are using most and gets rid of the ones we are not using. *I have always found neural pruning in adolescence fascinating, and I have my own theory about it. Have you noticed how the things that make you really happy in adulthood are usually the things you did as a teenager? The music you listen to, the hobbies and interests you have, even if you think about your favourite clothes, I can bet they will be related to your teenage self.* In individuals who have autism, the brain skips the pruning step (de Silva, 2018). This means that individuals with autism have more connection pathways in the brain, which could lead to hypersensitivity. This makes sense when we think about the sensory overwhelm that people with autism often experience.

When thinking about interpersonal relationships, contemporary research on autism has shown that, rather than autistic traits being unilateral, affecting all social interactions, problems arising in relationships could actually come from a mismatch in neurodivergent vs neurotypical cues. Individuals with autism process information from the world around them differently than neurotypical individuals, leading to what Milton et al. (2022) called "The Double Empathy Problem". Constructivism and Attachment Theory show us that to make emotional connections and communicate with others, we need to be able to predict how the interaction will proceed for safety and social cues. If both people in the dialogue are unable to predict what the other will do, then the information is misread and misunderstood. Communication becomes very difficult if you find it hard to understand what the other person is saying. However, we can imagine that if both people are viewing the world in similar ways, divergent + divergent or typical + typical, they can predict how each other will react, feel safe, and find ways to be together.

Attention Deficit Hyperactive Disorder (ADHD)

Using our ICAT framework, we will explore brain development along with attention and executive functioning challenges. When thinking about brain development, in ADHD, there are not only structural differences when compared with neurotypical brains, but there are also chemical differences. Research has shown (NIMH, 2007; Wang et al., 2021) that individuals with ADHD experience normal brain development, but it is delayed by around 3 years on average, with the prefrontal cortex (that area responsible for planning, decision-making and social inhibition) being most affected. The suggested 3-year delay indicates that individuals experiencing ADHD may present socially and in self-regulation as around 30% behind their chronological age. As the individual moves through chronological development and into adulthood, the differences in behaviours may appear reduced, especially as we can learn social rules to mask behaviours. The 30% delay may also explain why we see more pronounced behavioural challenges in children, rather than adults, as children develop complexity of thought and regulation quickly in neurotypical development and in contexts such as schools, children who are presenting with neurodivergent behaviours become more noticeable. When thinking about attention in ADHD, several networks within the brain, particularly the Default Mode Network, remain overly active instead of resting, which leads to individuals feeling like their mind never stops and is always wandering. This can also add to symptoms of cognitive delay as the individual may miss vital information in conversations, learning and the workplace, meaning that they miss social or task-oriented cues. Again, as in Autism, there is often heightened connectivity to all areas of the brain, especially as ADHD makes it hard for the brain to relax and rest, leading to increased sensory information being taken in and therefore having to be processed. The brain's energy is then consumed in processing surplus information, leaving little energy for filtering what is vital and what can make thinking and doing easier for the individual (Halbe et al., 2025).

Individuals with ADHD will also experience chemical changes in the brain, which will affect presenting behaviours. Dopamine is a chemical messenger which transmits messages of pleasure in the brain. Dopamine's scientific job is to support positive drive and motivation, anticipation and reinforce behaviours. For example, if we eat some food which is really tasty, the brain releases dopamine, and a neural pathway is created that links the tasty food with the good feeling of the dopamine chemical. If we are learning something and, as we say in England, "the penny drops" (it all works out well), dopamine spikes in the chemical makeup of the brain and a sense of reward and pride is felt. Dopamine is also required in our executive functioning processes, too. Executive functioning is like the CEO of our brains. It organises us, regulates, and makes decisions. Executive functioning stems from the prefrontal cortex area of the brain and is also in charge of our attention. If dopamine levels are out of sync, then our executive functioning skills become reduced, and we find it hard to choose, maintain attention or organise ourselves and our tasks. For individuals with ADHD, the dopamine pathways in the brain are often disrupted or underactive; therefore, the reward of completing a task, the ability to choose where to begin, or to focus attention on something is challenged. As the individual may not experience those natural highs when completing tasks, and as the body and brain often seek what they think they need subconsciously, individuals with ADHD will find ways to get that dopamine hit however they can. This can lead to risky behaviours, thrill-seeking and making decisions without thinking through the consequences, creating a feedback loop where the individual feels unsafe without the satiety.

ICAT Stance: *Adapt the relationship, not the nervous system.*

Within ICAT, neurodiversity invites a fundamental relational shift: rather than attempting to normalise nervous systems within therapy or "correct" difference, the practitioner adapts the relational environment to fit the individual's way of processing the world. Differences in sensory sensitivity, attention, language processing, and social prediction are understood as variations in how safety, meaning, and connection are organised, not as failures of attachment or motivation. For individuals with autism, relational difficulty is often rooted in mismatches of expectation and cue-reading rather than an absence of relational capacity, as described by the Double Empathy Problem. ICAT therefore slows pace, clarifies intention, reduces ambiguity, and privileges predictability over spontaneity, recognising that safety may be established through sameness, parallel activity, or shared interests rather than emotional expressiveness. Similarly, for individuals with ADHD, challenges in executive functioning, attention, and dopamine regulation are understood as shaping how engagement, anticipation, and regulation unfold in relationships. ICAT adapts by externalising structure, offering clear scaffolding, regulating rhythm, and reducing cognitive load, rather than interpreting distractibility or impulsivity as relational avoidance. Across both contexts, attachment security may be expressed through autonomy, movement, humour, or task-focused engagement rather than sustained verbal reflection. In this way, ICAT relocates responsibility from the individual to the relationship itself, protecting neurodivergent difference from being misread as resistance, pathology, or lack of capacity, and ensuring that relational work remains ethical, flexible, and responsive to diverse neurobiological organisations.

Alex, a 14-year-old autistic young person, was referred for therapy due to school refusal and increasing social withdrawal. Previous professionals described Alex as "unmotivated" and "resistant", noting limited eye contact, minimal verbal responses, and apparent disengagement during sessions. In early meetings, the ICAT-informed practitioner noticed that Alex became visibly tense when asked open-ended emotional questions and showed signs of sensory overload in the brightly lit room.

Rather than increasing emotional focus or interpreting withdrawal as avoidance, the practitioner adapted the relational environment. Sessions were shortened and held in a quieter space with consistent seating and a predictable structure. Conversation initially centred on Alex's special interest in graphic design, with long pauses accepted and eye contact not expected. The practitioner used clear, concrete language and checked understanding without pressure.

Over time, Alex began bringing drawings to sessions and using them to communicate experiences of overwhelm at school. Emotional understanding emerged indirectly through shared activity rather than direct questioning. As predictability and sensory safety increased, Alex's engagement became more sustained, and moments of reflection gradually appeared without being forced. Within ICAT, change occurred not because Alex was required to "open up", but because the relationship had been shaped to meet Alex's neurobiological and relational needs, allowing safety and meaning-making to develop at a tolerable pace.

Trauma and Survival-Organised Systems

ICAT Stance: Attachment strategies intensify under threat.

In ICAT-informed practice, trauma is not understood as a historical event that has failed to be integrated, but as an organising condition that continues to shape perception, anticipation, and relational behaviour in the present. In chronically traumatised individuals and systems, attachment strategies are not outdated patterns awaiting revision; they are current, active responses to ongoing or anticipated danger. What may appear rigid, exaggerated, or maladaptive from the outside often represents the most reliable means the individual has found to survive in contexts where safety has been inconsistent, conditional, or absent. ICAT therefore approaches trauma not by accelerating insight or challenging meaning, but by slowing relational pace and prioritising protection, predictability, and containment. In these contexts, relational work must adapt to survival rather than attempt to override it.

Hypervigilance as Intelligence

Within survival-organised systems, hypervigilance is often a refined skill rather than a symptom to be reduced. Individuals who have grown up in unpredictable or dangerous environments learn to constantly scan for changes in tone, posture, timing, or mood in others. This heightened sensitivity reflects an intelligence shaped by necessity: the ability to detect threat early in order to minimise harm. ICAT resists interpreting hypervigilance as paranoia or over-reaction, recognising instead that it is rooted in accurate historical learning. Attempting to reassure or rationalise away these perceptions too quickly can inadvertently increase danger by dismissing the individual's lived experience.

Dissociation as Protection

Dissociation is similarly understood within ICAT as a protective response rather than a lack of engagement. When emotional, relational, or sensory input exceeds the nervous system's capacity to cope, withdrawal from awareness may be the only available means of survival. In such moments, presence matters more than meaning. Attempts to explore feelings, reflect on causes, or link past and present may intensify the threat rather than relieve it. ICAT therefore prioritises grounding, rhythm, and relational steadiness, allowing contact with experience to return gradually and on the individual's terms.

Control as Safety-Seeking

In trauma-organised systems, control often replaces trust. Efforts to manage people, environments, or outcomes may appear oppositional or manipulative, but within ICAT, they are understood as attempts to create predictability where none has previously existed. Relinquishing control can feel equivalent to exposure, helplessness, or harm. For this reason, interventions that focus on compliance, flexibility, or emotional openness may be experienced as dangerous rather than supportive. ICAT responds by offering consistency and transparency, allowing safety to be built externally before expecting it internally.

Why Insight Can Feel Dangerous

A central ethical position within ICAT is that insight is not inherently therapeutic. For individuals whose nervous systems remain organised around threat, reflective questioning can replicate earlier experiences of interrogation, blame, or intrusion. Asking "why" too soon may increase shame, activate defensive strategies, or lead to withdrawal and collapse. ICAT explicitly slows down in these moments, recognising that reflection must emerge from safety rather than precede it. The practitioner's task is not to make sense of trauma prematurely, but to remain reliably present until sense-making becomes possible.

ICAT in Trauma-Organised Contexts

In trauma-organised systems, ICAT shifts from exploration to containment. The practitioner privileges predictability over novelty, presence over interpretation, and regulation over reflection. Change is understood as emergent and non-linear, arising through repeated experiences of safety rather than through insight alone. By respecting the intelligence of survival strategies and resisting the urge to accelerate meaning-making, ICAT protects individuals from relational harm and preserves the possibility of change when conditions allow.

The Ahmed family were referred to services due to concerns about school non-attendance, frequent conflict, and escalating emotional outbursts from their two children, aged eight and eleven. Both parents had experienced prolonged exposure to domestic violence and housing instability, and the family were currently living under ongoing financial and legal stress. Previous interventions had focused on parenting strategies and emotional literacy, but these were repeatedly described by the parents as "too much" and "not helpful."

In early meetings, the ICAT-informed practitioner noticed that both parents appeared hypervigilant, frequently checking the practitioner's tone and responses for signs of judgment or threat. Attempts to explore feelings or reflect on the children's emotional needs led to increased agitation, defensive explanations, and occasional withdrawal from sessions. Rather than interpreting this as resistance, the practitioner understood the family's behaviour as evidence of a survival-organised system in which safety remained uncertain.

The practitioner slowed the work considerably, shifting focus away from insight-based intervention and toward relational stability. Sessions became predictable in structure and length, with clear explanations of purpose and no unexpected changes. Practical concerns were prioritised, including advocacy around housing and school communication, reducing immediate pressure on the family system. Emotional content was acknowledged but not pursued beyond what the parents could tolerate.

Over time, as the practitioner remained consistent and transparent, the family's nervous systems began to settle. Parents became less defensive, and moments of curiosity about the children's behaviour emerged spontaneously. Reflection developed gradually, not through questioning, but through repeated experiences of being met without judgment or urgency. Within ICAT, change occurred not because the family were asked to understand their trauma, but because the relational environment no longer required them to stay in survival mode.

Culture, Power, and Structural Constraint

ICAT stance: Some strategies are rational responses to injustice.

In ICAT-informed practice, relational strategies are never understood in isolation from the social and structural conditions in which they emerge. Attachment patterns and interpersonal constructs are shaped not only by early caregiving relationships, but by ongoing experiences of power, marginalisation, and constraint. Racism, poverty, migration, gendered violence, disability, and systemic surveillance all influence how safe it is to be visible, expressive, or emotionally open. In such contexts, strategies that may be interpreted as avoidance, compliance, emotional distance, or hypervigilance can represent adaptive responses to real and present risk.

In this instance, ICAT is not being applied through a culturally individualistic lens. Relational norms around closeness, autonomy, emotion, authority, and disclosure are culturally situated, and assumptions about what constitutes "healthy" attachment or reflective capacity often reflect dominant social values rather than universal truths. ICAT therefore resists interpreting difference as deficit and instead attends carefully to how meaning is co-constructed within unequal power structures.

From this perspective, silence may function as safety, distance as dignity, and compliance as protection rather than passivity. Individuals and families living under structural constraints often have limited relational choice; strategies that preserve access to housing, employment, legal status, or physical safety may come at the cost of emotional openness or relational risk-taking. ICAT recognises that asking individuals to revise these strategies without addressing the conditions that necessitate them risks re-enacting harm.

The ethical move within ICAT is therefore to shift responsibility away from the individual and toward the relational and institutional environments in which they are embedded. Practitioners are invited to reflect not only on attachment dynamics, but on their own positionality, authority, and the implicit power they carry. Relational work becomes an act of cultural humility, where curiosity replaces assumption and safety is negotiated rather than prescribed. Only when individuals experience their context as sufficiently respectful and predictable does relational exploration become possible.

Amina, a 32-year-old woman, was referred to a community mental health service due to persistent anxiety and social withdrawal. She had migrated to the UK after fleeing political violence and was living with ongoing uncertainty regarding her immigration status. Previous professionals described her as "disengaged" and "overly compliant", noting limited emotional expression and a tendency to agree quickly with recommendations.

In early sessions, the ICAT-informed practitioner noticed that Amina avoided eye contact, spoke cautiously, and frequently checked whether her responses were "correct". Rather than interpreting this as low insight or insecure attachment, the practitioner understood these behaviours as potentially protective strategies shaped by experiences of surveillance, authority, and risk. The practitioner explicitly acknowledged the power imbalance within the therapeutic relationship and invited Amina to set boundaries around what felt safe to discuss.

Initial work focused on practical support, including navigating services and clarifying rights, rather than emotional exploration. Language was kept clear and non-clinical, and assumptions about assertiveness or emotional openness were intentionally held back. Over time, as sessions remained predictable and respectful of cultural meaning-making, Amina began to share fears about visibility and the consequences of being misunderstood.

Reflection emerged gradually, not because her silence was challenged, but because it was recognised as a rational response to injustice. Within ICAT, relational change occurred through adaptation of the relational environment rather than pressure on the individual to conform to normative expectations of engagement.

When ICAT Must Slow Down or Step Aside

Core ethical statement: *The ethical use of ICAT includes knowing when not to use it.*

ICAT is a relational framework designed to support safety, reflection, and flexibility. It is not a universal intervention to be applied regardless of context, nor a technique to be used in the face of ongoing danger. An essential ethical position within ICAT is the recognition that there are moments—and entire systems—in which relational meaning-making is premature or unsafe. In such circumstances, attempting to explore attachment patterns or interpersonal constructs may increase distress, reinforce threat, or replicate earlier experiences of intrusion and powerlessness.

Within ICAT-informed practice, slowing down is not a failure of therapeutic intent but an act of relational responsibility. Signs that reflection may be premature include persistent physiological dysregulation, escalating crises, rigid or concrete thinking, dissociation, or repeated relational rupture. In these moments, the individual's nervous system remains organised around survival rather than exploration. Asking "why", encouraging insight, or inviting emotional disclosure may be experienced as overwhelming or coercive, even when well-intentioned.

This section, therefore, distinguishes between relational avoidance and relational unavailability. The former may soften with safety; the latter signals that safety has not yet been established. ICAT explicitly privileges presence over interpretation in such contexts. Holding, witnessing, and maintaining consistency become the work. Meaning-making is deferred, not abandoned, until the conditions for it exist.

There are also situations in which ICAT must step aside entirely. Acute safeguarding concerns, severe mental or physical illness, ongoing abuse, or profound material deprivation may require practical intervention, advocacy, or specialist services before relational work can proceed. Ethical practice involves recognising when one's role is no longer to explore meaning, but to help reduce threat. This may include pausing therapy, facilitating referral, or supporting access to resources that restore basic safety.

Importantly, this stance also protects practitioners. Over-identification, role confusion, and relational over-reach are real risks in work with high levels of distress. ICAT does not ask practitioners to contain what cannot yet be contained or to remain relationally available at the expense of their own safety. Supervision, boundaries, and organisational support are integral to ethical restraint. Knowing when to pause, step back, or hand over responsibility is as vital as knowing when to lean in.

In this way, ICAT resists the pressure to produce insight or change on demand. It affirms that readiness is relational, contextual, and time-dependent. By respecting the limits of what is possible in the present moment, ICAT preserves the possibility of future work that is safer, deeper, and more genuinely transformative.

James, a 41-year-old man, was referred for therapy following a series of relationship breakdowns and increasing alcohol use. During early sessions, he appeared emotionally volatile, alternating between intense disclosure and abrupt withdrawal. He reported ongoing legal proceedings related to domestic conflict and was living in unstable housing.

The ICAT-informed practitioner initially attempted gentle exploration of relational patterns, but noticed that reflective questions led to rapid escalation, dissociation, and missed appointments. Rather than intensifying engagement or interpreting this as resistance, the practitioner recognised that James's nervous system remained organised around immediate threat.

The work was deliberately slowed. Sessions became shorter and more structured, with a focus on grounding and practical planning rather than emotional exploration. The practitioner supported James to engage with housing services and legal advocacy and maintained clear boundaries around session content and availability. When alcohol use increased, the practitioner facilitated a referral to specialist services rather than attempting to process the underlying meaning prematurely.

Over time, as James's external circumstances stabilised, his capacity for reflection increased. Relational work resumed gradually, with greater tolerance for uncertainty and emotional proximity. Within ICAT, change occurred not because insight was forced, but because the practitioner recognised when stepping back was the most ethical and relationally attuned response.

Across the contexts explored in this chapter—neurobiological difference, trauma, culture, power, and moments where intervention must pause—a consistent principle emerges: meaningful relational change cannot be compelled, but must be prepared for. Within ICAT, this preparation rests not on insight or technique, but on the cumulative experience of safety, predictability, and consistency over time. Safety allows the nervous system to settle; predictability reduces the need for vigilance; and consistency builds the trust required for flexibility and reflection to emerge. When these conditions are reliably present, attachment strategies soften, constructs become more permeable, and new meanings can be tentatively explored. When they are absent, slowing down or stepping aside becomes an ethical necessity rather than a missed opportunity. ICAT does not force readiness or define progress by speed. Instead, it honours the reality that change unfolds when relational conditions allow, and that waiting—when done with presence and care—is itself a profound therapeutic act.

Chapter 10
Closing Remarks

These final words are concerned with readiness. Not readiness as motivation, compliance, or insight, but readiness as a relational state that emerges when conditions allow. Throughout this book, ICAT has been presented not as a technique-driven model, but as a way of understanding how attachment, meaning-making, and context interact to shape what is possible between people. This chapter brings those strands together by focusing on how relational capacity is restored once safety has been compromised, and how practitioners can support this process without urgency or force.

Relational change does not begin with interpretation. It begins with a shift from constraint to capacity. Where threat, trauma, difference, or injustice have narrowed relational possibility, the task is not to challenge strategies or accelerate insight, but to rebuild the conditions in which thinking, feeling, and connection can re-emerge. Within ICAT, patience is therefore not a passive stance; it is an intervention in its own right. Waiting, when done with presence and consistency, communicates safety more powerfully than explanation ever could.

Across contexts, the rebuilding of relational capacity relies on the same foundational elements: holding, rhythm, and predictability. Repetition allows the nervous system to learn that experiences are not random. Reliability enables anticipation without vigilance. Environmental consistency reduces cognitive and emotional load, freeing energy for engagement. These elements do not demand change from the individual; they create a landscape in which change becomes possible.

As safety begins to stabilise, re-entry into a relationship often occurs through micro-attunements rather than significant emotional breakthroughs. Small moments matter. A shared glance, a brief smile, parallel activity, or a low-demand interaction can re-establish connection without overwhelming the system. ICAT attends closely to these moments, recognising that shared experience often precedes shared meaning.

Crucially, regulation must be supported before meaning-making is invited. This includes attention to the body, sensory experience, and co-regulation within

R. Swanick, *A Clinical Guide to Interpersonal Constructs and Attachment Theory*, https://doi.org/10.1007/978-3-032-23728-6_10

relationships. Whether through rhythm, movement, grounding, or simply being alongside another without expectation, regulation creates the conditions for reflection. Insight that arrives before regulation risks re-enacting threat; insight that follows regulation feels earned, tolerable, and safe.

Over time, signs of readiness begin to appear. Curiosity returns, not as interrogation but as interest. Playfulness and humour re-emerge, signalling flexibility. Rigid patterns soften. The system begins to tolerate uncertainty and novelty without collapse. These are not outcomes to be engineered; they are indicators that the relational environment has become safe enough to support growth.

Revisiting the ICAT Model

At its core, ICAT integrates attachment theory and constructivist thought to offer a relational account of human behaviour. Attachment strategies are understood as adaptive responses to safety and threat. Interpersonal constructs organise meaning and anticipation, shaping how individuals interpret and respond to relational experience. Neither operates in isolation. Both are continuously influenced by context, culture, neurobiology, and power.

ICAT resists pathologising behaviour and instead asks a consistent orienting question: *What does this relational system need right now to make thinking possible?* Sometimes the answer is attunement. Sometimes it is containment. Sometimes it is slowing down, stepping back, or addressing practical realities before relational work can proceed. Change is not produced through technique, but through relationship.

By positioning practitioners as participants within relational systems—rather than neutral observers—ICAT emphasises responsibility without blame. Our presence, pacing, boundaries, and assumptions shape the work as much as any intervention. This is not a model that promises certainty or control. It is one that asks for attentiveness, flexibility, and ethical restraint.

Hope, Humility, and Relational Responsibility

This book has argued repeatedly that people do not fail to change because they are resistant, unmotivated, or incapable. More often, they are protecting themselves in contexts that have not yet felt safe enough. The hope within ICAT lies not in optimism or outcome, but in the quiet confidence that relational systems can reorganise when conditions allow.

Humility is therefore essential. Practitioners do not decide when another is ready. We do not manufacture insight or demand openness. Our task is to notice, to wait, and to respond carefully when readiness begins to show itself. This requires tolerating uncertainty, resisting urgency, and trusting relational processes that unfold over time.

Relational responsibility sits at the heart of ICAT. Every interaction is an opportunity to reinforce safety or to undermine it. Every moment of consistency, repair, and attunement contributes to the conditions for change. We cannot always remove threat, injustice, or difference, but we can refuse to add to them through misattunement, haste, or assumption.

In this way, ICAT is not simply a framework for practice, but a stance towards others—and towards ourselves. It asks us to remain present, patient, and responsive, even when progress is slow or unclear. It reminds us that restoring the conditions for relational change is not an abstract goal, but a deeply human task, carried out one relationship at a time.

This book has grown out of many years of working alongside children, adults, families, students, and professionals in moments of distress, uncertainty, and hope. Again and again, I have been reminded that behaviour makes sense when we understand the conditions in which it emerged, and that change becomes possible not through pressure or perfection, but through relationships that are steady, thoughtful, and human. ICAT reflects both theory and lived experience, shaped by what clients, learners, and colleagues have taught me about safety, meaning, and survival. If there is one thing I hope this book offers, it is permission—to slow down, to stay curious, and to trust that being reliably present can matter more than getting it right.

Relational change does not arrive because we insist upon it, but because, over time, someone has been met with enough safety, patience, and consistency to risk being known.

Chapter 11
Case Studies in ICAT Practice: Introduction and Orientation

The case studies in this chapter are intended to bring the ICAT framework to life across a range of professional contexts, including therapy, education, social care, residential settings, adult learning, and community mental health. Rather than presenting idealised or exemplary practice, they focus on *ordinary moments of relational decision-making* in which attachment strategies and interpersonal constructs become visible, active, and open to change.

Each case has been selected to illustrate how ICAT operates as a **relational practice rather than a set of techniques**. The emphasis throughout is on process rather than outcome, and on how safety, attunement, and meaning-making are negotiated moment-to-moment within real-world constraints. The cases deliberately avoid linear narratives of progress, instead highlighting the iterative nature of relational work, where advances, pauses, and repairs coexist.

Across the examples, behaviour is consistently understood as **adaptive and informative**, shaped by histories of safety and threat rather than by fixed traits or deficits. Presenting difficulties are therefore explored in terms of their function within particular relational systems, whether those systems are dyadic, familial, institutional, cultural, or structural. In this way, the case studies reflect the core ICAT position that attachment strategies and interpersonal constructs are intelligible responses to lived experience, even when they become limiting in new contexts.

Each case follows a common structure: background context, an ICAT-informed formulation, selected relational interventions, and reflective questions for practitioners. This structure is intended to support readers in developing their own relational judgement rather than encouraging replication. The reflective questions are not assessment tools, but invitations to consider how similar dynamics may appear in one's own practice, and how professional positioning, pacing, and ethical awareness shape what becomes possible.

Importantly, the cases span the lifespan and a range of systems in order to demonstrate that ICAT is not confined to therapeutic settings. Whether the practitioner is a therapist, teacher, social worker, key worker, tutor, or support professional, the

R. Swanick, *A Clinical Guide to Interpersonal Constructs and Attachment Theory*, https://doi.org/10.1007/978-3-032-23728-6_11

same relational principles apply: regulation precedes reflection, meaning emerges through relationship, and change depends on safety over time.

Learning Through Difficulty: The Role of "What Went Wrong" Cases

The second part of the chapter intentionally shifts focus from examples of effective practice to situations in which relational work breaks down, becomes stuck, or inadvertently causes harm. These "What Went Wrong" cases are a central component of the ICAT framework, reflecting the belief that ethical practice is strengthened not by perfection, but by reflective engagement with difficulty.

Rather than attributing these breakdowns to practitioner incompetence or client resistance, the cases explore how misattunement, premature interpretation, unexamined assumptions, systemic pressure, or organisational constraint can narrow relational possibilities. In each example, the ICAT analysis highlights where safety was compromised, where meaning-making was imposed rather than explored, or where professional authority became either overused or avoided.

These cases serve a dual purpose. First, they protect ICAT from misuse by making explicit the risks of applying relational or reflective approaches without sufficient attention to context, culture, neurobiology, or power. Second, they offer practitioners permission to acknowledge uncertainty, error, and limitation as inherent to relational work. Within ICAT, recognising when an approach is not working—or should not yet be used—is understood as an ethical strength rather than a failure.

The optional reflection questions that accompany these cases are designed to support supervision, training, and individual reflection. They invite practitioners to consider not only alternative responses, but also the systemic and organisational pressures that shape practice, and the emotional impact of this work on professionals themselves.

Summary

Taken together, the case studies in this chapter demonstrate that ICAT is less about *doing something to* individuals and more about *being with* them in ways that support safety, curiosity, and flexibility. Across contexts, change emerges not through insight alone, but through repeated experiences of attuned, predictable, and reparative relationships.

The cases show that ICAT techniques are most effective when they are used sparingly, responsively, and in relation to what the present moment allows. They also illustrate that there are times when ICAT must slow down, adapt, or step aside in favour of holding, advocacy, or systemic intervention. Knowing when and how to do this is a central ethical responsibility of ICAT-informed practice.

By grounding theory in lived relational encounters—including moments of success, uncertainty, and failure—this chapter aims to support practitioners in developing confidence not in techniques, but in relational judgement. In doing so, it reinforces the core ICAT proposition that meaningful change occurs through relationships that make thinking possible, without forcing it.

Case Study 1: Therapy

Reconstructing Safety in Adult Attachment

Background

Client: Sarah, 34

Presenting issue: Chronic relationship anxiety, fear of abandonment, emotional overwhelm

History: Multiple unstable caregiving relationships in childhood, periods of emotional neglect

Attachment pattern (DMM-informed): Anxious/preoccupied with disorganised elements

Core constructs:

- *"If I am not needed, I will be left"*
- *"Strong feelings push people away"*
- *"I must monitor others constantly to stay safe"*

Sarah frequently contacted her therapist between sessions, became distressed when boundaries were maintained, and interpreted neutral responses as rejection.

ICAT Formulation

Attachment Loop

- Trigger: Partner delayed replying to a message
- Prediction: *"He is losing interest"*
- Affect: Panic, shame
- Behaviour: Repeated texting, emotional withdrawal
- Outcome: Relationship tension → reinforces belief

Construct System

- Core polarity: *Connection* vs. *Abandonment*
- Peripheral construct: *Independence = Danger*
- Family narrative: "Women in our family are always left"

Intervention

1. Affect Attunement

The therapist consistently named and validated emotional states:

> It sounds like in that moment it felt frighteningly lonely, almost like you were invisible.

This reduced defensive escalation and strengthened therapeutic attachment.

2. Mentalisation

Sessions focused on reflective questioning:

What do you imagine might have been happening for him at that moment?

How did you understand his silence?

Gradually, Sarah learned to hold multiple interpretations.

3. Reconstructing Constructs (Kelly)

Using laddering:

- "What does it mean if he doesn't reply?" → "I'm unimportant"
- "If you're unimportant, then what?" → "I'll be alone forever"

This exposed the core construct.

Alternative construals were collaboratively developed:

- "Delay ≠ rejection"
- "I can tolerate uncertainty"

4. MKO Interruption

Therapist deliberately slowed responses to between-session emails (within ethical boundaries), modelling stable presence without over-rescuing. This disrupted the habitual reassurance loop.

Outcome

Over 18 months, Sarah:

- Reduced reassurance-seeking
- Reported improved emotional regulation
- Formed a more secure romantic relationship
- Developed reflective capacity around attachment triggers

She described feeling "less ruled by panic and more able to choose how I respond".

Case Study 1 (Therapy): Reflective Questions

Reconstructing Safety in Adult Attachment

Attachment & Emotional Regulation

1. What attachment strategies did Sarah use to manage perceived relational threat?
2. How did her early relational experiences shape her expectations of intimacy?
3. In what ways did her emotional responses make sense within her attachment history?

Meaning-Making & Constructs

4. What core and peripheral constructs organised Sarah's understanding of relationships?
5. How did these constructs influence her interpretations of ambiguous situations?
6. Which constructs appeared most resistant to change, and why?

Practitioner Positioning

7. How did the therapist's responses contribute to a secure therapeutic base?
8. When did the therapist act as a "More Knowledgeable Other" within the ICAT cycle?
9. How was therapeutic pacing used to avoid reinforcing dependency?

Mentalisation & Attunement

10. How was reflective functioning fostered in moments of high affect?
11. What risks might arise if mentalisation is introduced too quickly?
12. How did affect attunement support cognitive change?

Application to Practice

13. How might you recognise similar attachment–construct cycles in your own clients?
14. What boundaries are necessary when working with anxious attachment?
15. How would you adapt this approach for short-term therapy contexts?

Case Study 2: Education

<u>Supporting Emotional Security in the Classroom</u>

<u>Background</u>

Student: Daniel, 9

Context: Primary school

Presenting issues: Disruptive behaviour, refusal to complete work, frequent outbursts

History: Parental separation, inconsistent caregiving

Attachment strategy: Avoidant-defensive with controlling tendencies

Teacher reports: "He doesn't care and just wants attention"

ICAT Formulation

Attachment Loop

- Trigger: Teacher corrects work
- Prediction: *"I'm stupid/I'll be shamed"*
- Affect: Anxiety masked as anger
- Behaviour: Disruption, withdrawal
- Outcome: Sanctions → reinforces self-concept

Construct System

- *Competent* vs. *Worthless*
- *Control* vs. *Humiliation*
- Learning = Risk

Family narrative: "You have to be tough; no one helps you".

Intervention

1. Teacher as MKO

Teacher trained in attachment-informed practice. Instead of public correction, she began using private feedback and predictable routines.

2. Affect Attunement in Learning

When Daniel escalated:

It looks like that felt really hard just now. Let's slow down.

This replaced punitive responses.

3. Scaffolding (Vygotsky)

Work broken into achievable steps with immediate feedback. Daniel was positioned in the ZPD with consistent support.

4. Construct Reconstruction

Through reflective conversations:

Teacher: "What goes through your mind when work feels tricky?"

Daniel: "Everyone thinks I'm dumb".

Alternative narrative developed:

- "Struggling means learning"
- "Mistakes are information"

5. Relational Consistency

Teacher greeted Daniel daily, maintained calm tone, repaired ruptures. This built a secure base.

Outcome

After two terms:

- Behaviour incidents reduced
- Literacy scores improved
- Increased classroom participation
- Daniel began requesting help appropriately

He later stated, "Miss doesn't give up on me".

Case Study 2 (Education): Reflective Questions

<u>Supporting Emotional Security in the Classroom</u>

Attachment in Learning

1. How did Daniel's attachment strategy influence his learning behaviour?
2. In what ways did classroom interactions activate threat responses?
3. How might misinterpretation of his behaviour reinforce insecurity?

Construction of Meaning

4. What meanings had Daniel constructed around "ability" and "mistakes"?
5. How were these meanings socially reinforced within the school environment?
6. How did language used by adults influence his self-concept?

Teacher as MKO

7. How did the teacher function as a secure base for exploration?
8. Which specific practices disrupted Daniel's habitual response patterns?
9. How can educators balance emotional support with academic expectations?

Attunement & Regulation

10. How did emotional co-regulation precede cognitive engagement?
11. What signs indicated that Daniel was becoming more regulated?
12. How might attunement differ for students with different attachment styles?

Application to Practice

13. How could this approach be implemented in larger classrooms?
14. What systemic barriers might limit relational work in schools?
15. How can schools support staff to maintain reflective capacity?

Case Study 3: Social Care

Changing Family Narratives in Child Protection

Background

Family: The Jacksons
Parents: Mark (38), Leanne (35)
Children: Amy (7), Jake (4)
Referral: Neglect concerns, school non-attendance, emotional volatility
History: Both parents experienced childhood trauma and care placements
Attachment pattern: Intergenerational insecure/disorganised
Family construct system:

- *Authorities = Threat*
- *Asking for help = Weakness*
- *We must survive alone*

ICAT Formulation

Systemic Attachment Loop

- Professional visits → fear
- Prediction: "They'll take our kids"
- Affect: Shame, rage
- Behaviour: Missed appointments, hostility
- Outcome: Increased monitoring

Family Plot (Ugazio)

- Mark = Protector
- Leanne = Overwhelmed Carer
- Professionals = Enemies

Intervention

1. Relationship Before Regulation

Key worker prioritised trust:

> My job is to help you keep your family together safely.

Consistent visits, transparency, no surprises.

2. Affect Attunement

Acknowledged parental fear:

> Anyone with your experiences would be terrified of us.

Reduced defensiveness.

3. Mentalisation-Based Work

Exploring children's perspectives:

What do you think Amy feels when mornings are rushed?

Parents gradually reflected on the emotional impact.

4. Family Construct Mapping

Using adapted laddering:

- "Why avoid school?" → "They judge us"
- "If judged?" → "We'll lose everything"

Core threat construct identified.

5. Re-authoring Narrative

Collaborative reframing:

- "Support = Protection"
- "Working together = Strength"

Parents are involved in planning.

6. MKO Interruption

Key worker modelled calm problem-solving during crises rather than escalation.

Outcome

Within 12 months:

- Improved school attendance
- Safer home routine
- Reduced safeguarding level
- Parents engaged voluntarily with support services

Leanne stated: "For the first time, it feels like someone's on our side".

Case Study 3 (Social Care): Reflective Questions

<u>Changing Family Narratives in Child Protection</u>

Systemic Attachment Patterns

1. How did intergenerational attachment patterns influence family functioning?
2. In what ways did fear shape parental engagement with services?
3. How did professional systems unintentionally reinforce insecurity?

Family Constructs & Narratives

4. What dominant "family plots" organised the Jacksons' interactions?
5. How did these narratives protect the family emotionally?
6. Which constructs need to change for sustainable improvement?

Professional Positioning

7. How did the key worker establish trust without colluding with risk?
8. What ethical tensions arose between safeguarding and relationship-building?
9. How was authority exercised in a relationally sensitive way?

Mentalisation in Parenting

10. How was parental reflective functioning supported?
11. What role did shame play in limiting parental insight?
12. How did increased mentalisation affect caregiving behaviour?

Application to Practice

13. How can professionals remain emotionally available in high-risk cases?
14. What organisational cultures support ICAT-informed work?
15. How can families be engaged as collaborators rather than subjects?

Case Study 4: Adolescent Therapy

From Emotional Shutdown to Relational Engagement.

Background

Client: Liam, 15

Presenting Issues: Social withdrawal, school refusal, low mood

History: Parental conflict, emotionally unavailable father, anxious mother

Attachment Strategy: Avoidant–dismissive

Core Constructs:

- "Needing others is weak"
- "Feelings cause problems"
- "If I stay quiet, I'm safe"

Liam attended therapy reluctantly and responded minimally.

ICAT Formulation

Attachment Loop

- Trigger: Emotional questioning
- Prediction: "I'll be judged"
- Affect: Anxiety → numbness
- Behaviour: Silence, disengagement
- Outcome: Adult backs off → reinforces avoidance

Construct Polarity:

Independence vs. Vulnerability

Intervention

1. Affect Attunement

Therapist respected silence, naming it gently:

Sometimes being quiet feels safer than talking.

2. Mentalisation

Used third-person reflection (films, stories) before self-focus.

3. Construct Work

Explored masculinity narratives in family culture.

4. MKO Disruption

Therapist maintained a consistent interest without pressure.

Outcome

After 9 months, Liam initiated conversations, returned to school part-time, and reported feeling "less invisible".

Case Study 4 (Adolescent Therapy—Liam)
Attachment & Development

1. How did Liam's avoidant strategy function as protection?
2. What risks might arise if emotional expression is pushed too early?
3. How did the developmental stage influence intervention choices?

Meaning & Identity

4. How did gender and cultural narratives shape Liam's constructs?
5. What meanings did he attach to vulnerability?
6. How were these gently challenged?

Therapeutic Positioning

7. How did the therapist balance patience with therapeutic intent?
8. What might "over-activity" have communicated to Liam?
9. How did consistency function as an intervention?

Application

10. How would you work with resistance without pathologising it?
11. How might this approach differ in brief services?
12. What indicators suggest readiness for deeper work?

Case Study 5: Early Years & Parenting Support
<u>Building Secure Foundations in Young Families.</u>

<u>Background</u>
Parent: Nadia, 22
Child: Yusuf, 18 months
Context: Community health visiting
Concerns: Limited eye contact, inconsistent responsiveness
History: Nadia grew up in foster care
Attachment Pattern: Fearful–avoidant
Constructs:

- "Babies manipulate"
- "Getting close leads to loss"

ICAT Formulation
Attachment Loop

- Trigger: Child crying
- Prediction: "I'm failing"
- Affect: Panic
- Behaviour: Withdrawal
- Outcome: Child escalates

Construct Polarity:
Closeness vs. Overwhelm
Intervention
1. Video Interaction Guidance (VIG)
Highlighted moments of attunement.
2. Affect Coaching
Named both Nadia's and Yusuf's emotions.
3. Mentalisation
Linked behaviour to needs.
4. MKO Role
Practitioner modelled soothing strategies.
Outcome
Increased sensitivity, improved bonding, secure base behaviours emerging.

Case Study 5 (Early Years—Nadia & Yusuf)
Attachment Formation

1. How did Nadia's history affect her caregiving responses?
2. What intergenerational patterns were visible?
3. How was safety built for both parent and child?

Constructs & Parenting

4. How did Nadia interpret Yusuf's behaviour?
5. Which beliefs inhibited responsiveness?
6. How were alternative meanings co-created?

Practitioner Skills

7. Why was video feedback particularly effective here?
8. How did the practitioner avoid shame-based intervention?
9. How was hope cultivated?

Application

10. How can this approach be adapted in high-caseload settings?
11. What ethical issues arise in home-based work?
12. How would you respond to parental disengagement?

Case Study 6: Residential Care Setting
Transforming Institutional Attachment Patterns.
Background
Setting: Residential children's home
Young Person: Kai, 13
History: Multiple placements, trauma
Behaviour: Aggression, absconding
Attachment Strategy: Controlling–disorganised
Group Construct:

- "Staff always leave"

- "Only power keeps you safe"

ICAT Formulation
Systemic Loop

- Trigger: Boundary setting
- Prediction: "I'll be abandoned"
- Affect: Rage
- Behaviour: Violence
- Outcome: Exclusion

Institutional Construct:
Control = Safety
Intervention
1. Team Reflective Practice
Used ICAT mapping in staff meetings.
2. Consistency Policy
Reduced staff changes.
3. Attunement Training
Emotion coaching.
4. MKO Interruption
Key worker stayed present during the crises.
Outcome
Reduced incidents, increased trust, improved school engagement.

Case Study 6 (Residential Care—Kai)
Systemic Attachment

1. How did institutional practices mirror Kai's attachment trauma?
2. What systemic anxieties were present?
3. How did staff turnover affect relational safety?

Group Constructs

4. What shared meanings maintained control-based practice?
5. How were these challenged organisationally?
6. How did leadership influence outcomes?

Professional Resilience

7. How did staff manage emotional exhaustion?
8. What risks arise when fear drives policy?
9. How was reflective space protected?

Application

10. How can ICAT inform organisational culture?
11. How would you respond to risk-averse management?
12. What structures support relational continuity?

Case Study 7: Adult Learning & Workforce Development

Re-engaging the Reluctant Learner.

Background

Learner: Paul, 47

Context: Vocational retraining

Issues: Avoids assessment, high anxiety

History: School failure, ridicule

Attachment Style: Avoidant–anxious

Constructs:

- "Education humiliates"
- "I'm not academic"

ICAT Formulation

Learning Loop

- Trigger: Testing
- Prediction: "I'll fail"
- Affect: Shame
- Behaviour: Procrastination
- Outcome: Poor results

Intervention

1. Narrative Reframing

Explored past learning trauma.

2. Scaffolded Assessment

Low-stakes practice.

3. Mentalisation

Normalised fear.

4. MKO Role

Tutor shared their own struggles.

Outcome

Course completion, increased confidence, and peer mentoring.

Case Study 7 (Adult Learning—Paul)

Learning & Shame

1. How did past educational trauma affect current engagement?
2. What role did shame play in avoidance?
3. How was psychological safety established?

Construct Reconstruction

4. How were deficit narratives dismantled?
5. Why was low-stakes assessment important?
6. How was self-efficacy developed?

Tutor Role

7. How did self-disclosure function therapeutically?

8. When might this be inappropriate?
9. How did the tutor avoid rescuing?

Application

10. How can adult educators recognise hidden attachment needs?
11. How might digital learning environments alter this work?
12. What systemic barriers exist?

Case Study 8: Community Mental Health & Migration

Negotiating Identity Across Cultures

Background

Client: Amina, 29
Context: Refugee mental health service
Issues: Anxiety, isolation
History: Forced displacement
Attachment Pattern: Fearful–preoccupied
Constructs:

- "Safety means invisibility"
- "Belonging is dangerous"

ICAT Formulation

Cultural–Attachment Loop

- Trigger: Social invitations
- Prediction: "I'll be exposed"
- Affect: Fear
- Behaviour: Avoidance
- Outcome: Loneliness

Intervention

1. Cultural Mentalisation
Explored identity narratives.
2. Group Therapy
Safe peer connection.
3. Affect Attunement
Validated trauma responses.
4. MKO Role
Therapist navigated systems.
Outcome
Increased social engagement, employment, improved wellbeing.

Case Study 8 (Migration & Mental Health—Amina)

Cultural Attachment

1. How did displacement affect attachment security?
2. How did culture shape emotional expression?
3. What risks exist in misinterpreting avoidance?

Identity & Meaning

4. How did Amina negotiate multiple identities?
5. What meanings were attached to visibility?
6. How were community narratives explored?

Professional Competence

7. How did the therapist demonstrate cultural humility?
8. What power dynamics were present?
9. How were systemic barriers addressed?

Application

10. How can services become more culturally responsive?
11. What role can peer support play?
12. How might immigration status affect engagement?

Part 2: "What Went Wrong?" ICAT Case Studies

The case studies that follow focus on moments where relational work did not proceed as intended, where interventions became misaligned with context, or where safety, meaning-making, or ethical positioning were compromised. These examples are not included to assign blame or to highlight poor practice. Rather, they reflect the reality that relational work is complex, emotionally demanding, and shaped by individual, systemic, and organisational pressures.

Within ICAT, moments of difficulty are understood as valuable sources of information. When work becomes stuck, escalates, or leads to disengagement, this often signals a mismatch between relational readiness and professional response, rather than a lack of motivation or capacity on the part of those involved. Examining such moments offers an opportunity to deepen understanding of attachment strategies, interpersonal constructs, and the conditions required for reflection to be possible.

These "What Went Wrong" cases are therefore an essential ethical component of the ICAT framework. They illustrate how well-intentioned interventions can inadvertently reinforce threat, shame, or power imbalance when timing, context, culture, or neurobiological regulation are not sufficiently considered. They also demonstrate the importance of recognising when relational approaches need to slow down, adapt, or be supplemented by other forms of support.

Readers are encouraged to approach these cases with curiosity rather than judgement, using them as prompts for reflection on their own practice contexts, constraints, and decision-making processes. In ICAT-informed work, the capacity to notice misalignment, repair errors, and revise one's approach is not a sign of failure, but a marker of ethical and relational competence.

<u>What Went Wrong 1: Over-Interpreting Avoidance</u>

<u>Context: Adolescent Therapy</u>

Client: Josh, 16

Issue: Withdrawal and silence

What Happened: The therapist interpreted silence as "defence" and repeatedly encouraged emotional disclosure. Josh felt exposed and stopped attending.

ICAT Analysis

Domain	Problem
Attachment	Avoidance not respected
Affect	Dysregulation ignored
Mentalisation	Assumptions replaced curiosity
MKO role	Became intrusive

Learning Points

- Safety precedes insight
- Silence may be regulation
- Pacing is attachment-informed care

What Went Wrong 2: Behaviour Without Meaning

Context: Primary School

Student: Mia, 7

Issue: Aggression

What Happened: The school implemented behaviour charts and exclusions. Aggression escalated.

ICAT Analysis

Domain	Problem
Constructs	Behaviour seen as defiance
Attachment	Fear ignored
System	Punitive loop reinforced

Learning Points

- Behaviour is communication
- Systems create meaning
- Regulation before compliance

What Went Wrong 3: Collusion in Social Care

Context: Child Protection

Family: Rahman Family

What Happened: The social worker avoided challenging unsafe routines to preserve rapport. Risk increased.

ICAT Analysis

Domain	Problem
MKO role	Avoided authority
Ethics	Safety compromised
Attachment	Fear of rejection

Learning Points

- Relationship ≠ avoidance
- Safety is relational
- Boundaries build trust

What Went Wrong 4: Cultural Misattunement

Context: Adult Therapy

Client: Mei, 31

What Happened: The therapist encouraged assertiveness without a cultural context. Client disengaged.

ICAT Analysis

Domain	Problem
Mentalisation	Cultural biases
Constructs	Western individualism imposed
Power	Unexamined authority

Learning Points

- Culture shapes attachment
- One model does not fit all
- Humility is competence

What Went Wrong 5: Burnout in Residential Care

Context: Care Home Staff

What Happened: Staff became emotionally detached due to the workload. Relationships deteriorated.

ICAT Analysis

Domain	Problem
System	No reflective space
Affect	Chronic suppression
Attachment	Institutional avoidance

Learning Points

- Staff need attachment too
- Reflection prevents burnout
- Organisational care matters

Optional Reflection Questions for "What Went Wrong" Cases
Critical Reflection

1. Where did the cycle first become rigid?
2. What alternative responses were available?
3. What systemic pressures were operating?
4. How might ICAT have redirected practice?
5. What would I do differently?

Appendix 1: Key ICAT Techniques

Practice Examples and Clarifications

The following examples are intended to illustrate how ICAT techniques may appear in practice. They are *illustrative rather than prescriptive*, and are offered to support practitioner judgement rather than replace it. Each example demonstrates a possible relational move, not a required intervention.

Attunement (Affect, Rhythm, and Vitality)

Practice Examples

- A therapist notices a client's speech quickening and their breathing becoming shallow when discussing family. The therapist slows their own pace, lowers their voice, and introduces longer pauses, signalling regulation rather than urgency.
- A teacher observes a child becoming increasingly restless during a task. Rather than insisting on completion, the teacher acknowledges the child's discomfort and adjusts expectations, allowing movement or a brief pause.
- A social worker senses emotional withdrawal during a home visit and responds by softening posture and reducing the number of questions, prioritising presence over information gathering.

What This Is Not

- Not simply being "nice" or agreeable
- Not constant validation of all feelings or behaviours
- Not ignoring risk, boundaries, or professional responsibility
- Not assuming attunement is achieved once and for all

R. Swanick, *A Clinical Guide to Interpersonal Constructs and Attachment Theory*, https://doi.org/10.1007/978-3-032-23728-6

Attunement is an ongoing, responsive process that includes noticing when it has been lost.

Marked Mirroring

Practice Examples

- A practitioner reflects, "It sounds like there's a lot of frustration there—almost as if things feel unfair right now", using tone and phrasing that recognises emotion without amplifying it.
- A parent support worker mirrors a caregiver's anxiety with calm curiosity, explicitly distinguishing between the adult's feelings and the child's needs.
- A therapist reflects sadness with warmth rather than distress, helping the client recognise emotion without becoming overwhelmed.

What This Is Not

- Not emotional mimicry or imitation
- Not intensifying or dramatising affect
- Not collapsing boundaries by "feeling it too much"
- Not using reflection to steer emotion in a desired direction

Marked mirroring maintains emotional differentiation while offering recognition.

Mentalising Dialogue

Practice Examples

- A therapist asks, "I'm wondering what might have gone through your mind when that happened—but I may be wrong", explicitly holding uncertainty.
- A teacher supports reflection by asking a student, "What do you think your friend might have felt in that moment?"
- A social care practitioner wonders aloud, "I notice I'm feeling a bit uncertain here—I wonder if that reflects how confusing this situation feels for everyone".

What This Is Not

- Not analysis disguised as curiosity
- Not pushing insight during high emotional arousal
- Not assuming rational reflection is always accessible
- Not correcting the client's interpretations

Mentalising dialogue invites reflection; it does not demand it.

Construct Exploration (Without Challenge)

Practice Examples

- A therapist asks, "What did you expect would happen when you spoke up?" rather than "That belief isn't accurate".
- A practitioner explores how a family understands "good parenting" without introducing alternative models too early.
- An educator invites a learner to reflect on how they define "success" and "failure", without reframing these concepts prematurely.

What This Is Not

- Not cognitive restructuring
- Not persuasion or debate
- Not identifying "distorted thinking"
- Not challenging protective beliefs before safety is established

Exploration honours the adaptive function of constructs before opening space for change.

Repair After Rupture

Practice Examples

- A therapist notices withdrawal after a comment and says, "I think I may have misunderstood something important—can we slow down and revisit that?"
- A teacher acknowledges a misstep: "I spoke too quickly earlier, and I can see that wasn't helpful".
- A social worker names tension following a difficult conversation and invites reflection on its impact.

What This is Not

- Not apologising excessively or collapsing authority
- Not avoiding necessary boundaries or decisions
- Not shifting responsibility onto the client
- Not assuming repair requires emotional disclosure

Repair models accountability, not self-doubt.

What ICAT Is Not (Overall)

To support ethical and consistent application, it is important to clarify what ICAT does *not* represent.

ICAT is not:

- A manualised intervention or step-by-step programme
- A technique-driven model detached from the relationship
- A replacement for safeguarding, risk assessment, or professional judgement
- A purely cognitive or purely emotional approach
- A model that assumes change should be fast or linear
- ICAT does not prioritise insight over safety, nor meaning over emotion. Instead, it holds these domains in constant interaction.

Integrative Clarification

ICAT techniques are best understood as *relational capacities* rather than tools to be applied. Their effectiveness depends on timing, context, and the practitioner's ability to remain emotionally present, reflective, and ethically grounded.

At different moments, the most therapeutic act may be:

- Slowing down rather than exploring
- Repairing rather than progressing
- Naming uncertainty rather than offering an explanation

This flexibility is not a limitation of ICAT, but one of its core strengths.

Appendix 2: ICAT Supporting Worksheets

The following worksheets are offered as reflective supports rather than assessment tools, designed to help practitioners remain grounded, curious, and ethically attuned when applying the ICAT framework in practice. They are intended to slow thinking rather than accelerate action, and to support relational judgement rather than replace it. The first worksheet is designed for individual practitioner reflection, offering prompts that orient attention toward safety, attachment strategies, interpersonal meaning, and the lived here-and-now of the relationship. The second is explicitly for supervision and consultation, recognising that practitioners themselves are part of the relational system and that their emotional, bodily, and cognitive responses carry important information. Used thoughtfully, these sheets can help practitioners notice when relational work is possible, when it needs to slow, and when holding or support for the practitioner must take priority over intervention.

R. Swanick, *A Clinical Guide to Interpersonal Constructs and Attachment Theory*, https://doi.org/10.1007/978-3-032-23728-6

1. Worksheet for Practitioners in Practice

ICAT Relational Reflection Worksheet

A practitioner prompt sheet for ethical, context-sensitive practice

ICAT orienting question:
What does this relational system need right now to make thinking possible?

This worksheet is designed to support reflective, relational decision-making.
It is **not** a diagnostic tool or a checklist.
Use selectively, slowly, and in supervision where possible.

1. Context & Current Conditions

(What is shaping this moment?)

Immediate context (life events, environment, systems):

____

____

Is there ongoing threat?
☐Yes (current) ☐Yes (remembered) ☐Unclear ☐No

What practical or environmental factors may need attention first?

____

____

____

2. Safety & Regulation

(Felt experience in the here and now)

Signs of relative safety (if present):
☐Calm breathing ☐Ability to stay present ☐Shared affect
☐Eye contact ☐Curiosity ☐Flexibility

Signs of threat or dysregulation:
☐Fight ☐Flight ☐Freeze ☐Dissociation ☐Hypervigilance
☐Emotional flooding ☐Rigidity ☐Withdrawal

What helps this person regulate (or what makes it harder)?

____

____

____

3. Attachment Strategies

(What is the behaviour doing?)

Observed relational patterns or strategies:
☐Avoidance / omission of affect
☐Intensification or distortion of affect

☐Control, oscillation, or collapse
☐Unclear / mixed

How might this behaviour be adaptive or protective?

What might happen if this strategy were unavailable right now?

---

4. Interpersonal Constructs & Meaning

(How experience is organised)

Key meanings, expectations, or narratives (spoken or implicit):

Possible core binaries (e.g. safe/dangerous, worthy/unworthy):

What does this person anticipate will happen next?

---

5. Here-and-Now Relational Information

(Live data from the interaction)

Notable shifts in the interaction (tone, pace, affect, engagement):

Moments of rupture, hesitation, or intensity:

What might this moment be communicating relationally?

---

6. Practitioner Positioning

(You are part of the system)

My internal responses (emotional, bodily, cognitive):

Any urges noticed?
☐Rescue ☐Explain ☐Reassure ☐Withdraw ☐Fix ☐Avoid conflict

What support do I need (supervision, pause, consultation)?

____

____

7. Relational Moves Available

(Not a sequence — a repertoire)

Which of the following might support safety *without foreclosing growth*?

☐Affect attunement
☐Marked mirroring
☐Mentalising dialogue
☐Gentle construct exploration
☐Naming and repairing rupture
☐Holding / waiting
☐Practical support or advocacy
☐Stepping back / referral

What feels most ethically appropriate right now?

____

____

8. When to Slow Down or Pause

(Ethical restraint)

Are there signs reflection is premature?
☐Increased distress ☐Shutdown ☐Heightened threat response
☐Insight feels dangerous ☐System remains survival-focused

If so, what does slowing down look like here?

____

____

____

Closing Reflection

One sentence to carry forward:

____

What does this system need *next* — not eventually, but next?

____

2. Worksheet for Practitioners in Supervision

ICAT Supervision Reflection Sheet

For use in supervision, consultation, or reflective practice groups

Supervisory orienting question:
What is being evoked in this relational system — and how am I positioned within it?

This reflection sheet is designed to support **ethical containment of the practitioner**, not to generate plans, formulations, or interventions.
It assumes that **the practitioner is part of the attachment–construct system** under consideration.

1. Case Snapshot (Minimal Detail)

Context / setting (therapy, education, health, social care, organisation):

Presenting concern (brief, behavioural description only):

Current level of risk or threat:
☐Low ☐Moderate ☐High ☐Unclear

---

2. What Is Happening Relationally?

Patterns I notice repeating (in sessions, meetings, contact):

Where do things tighten, escalate, stall, or collapse?

What feels most difficult to stay with?

---

3. Attachment & Strategy (Practitioner View)

Observed attachment strategies in the other:
☐Withdrawal / minimisation
☐Intensification / escalation
☐Control / oscillation
☐Disorganisation / collapse
☐Unclear

How do these strategies make sense in context?

What might these strategies be protecting against *right now*?

4. Construct Systems at Play

Key meanings or expectations organising the relationship:
(e.g. "I will be judged", "Authority is dangerous", "Needing is weak")

What predictions seem to be running the system?

What might *my* role represent within these constructs?

5. The Here-and-Now Field

What happens between us in real time?
(tone, pace, silences, urgency, compliance, withdrawal, intensity)

Moments I felt pulled to act (or stop acting):

6. Practitioner Internal Experience

(This is the heart of the sheet)

Emotional responses I notice in myself:
☐Anxiety ☐Urgency ☐Helplessness ☐Frustration
☐Sadness ☐Protectiveness ☐Irritation ☐Numbness
☐Confidence ☐Over-responsibility

Bodily signals:

Dominant urges:
☐Rescue ☐Explain ☐Fix ☐Reassure
☐Withdraw ☐Placate ☐Confront ☐Avoid

What might these responses be communicating about the system?

7. Safety, Ethics, and Pace

Is reflective work currently possible?
☐Yes ☐Partially ☐Not yet

If not, what is still missing?

☐Safety ☐Predictability ☐Containment
☐Practical stability ☐Trust ☐Time

Where might I be moving faster than the system allows?

Where might I be avoiding necessary authority or clarity?

---

8. Relational Responsibility (ICAT Lens)

What is *my* responsibility in this moment?
(not what I can fix, but what I can ethically hold)

What is *not* my responsibility here?

Do I need to:

☐Slow down
☐Reduce interpretation
☐Increase containment
☐Seek consultation
☐Advocate systemically
☐Pause or step back

---

9. Supervisory Integration

What feels clearer after reflection?

What still feels uncertain or unresolved?

One grounded next step (not an outcome):

Supervisory Note

ICAT supervision prioritises the regulation and reflective capacity of the practitioner. When the practitioner is supported to think, feel, and locate themselves within the relational field, ethical practice follows naturally. Supervision is not the place to perform competence, but to restore it.

References

Ainsworth, M. D. S. (1967). *Infancy in Uganda: Infant care and the growth of love*. Johns Hopkins Press.
Ainsworth, M. D., & Bell, S. M. (1970). Attachment, exploration, and separation: Illustrated by the behavior of one-year-olds in a strange situation. *Child Development, 41*(1), 49–67.
Ainsworth, M. D. S., Bell, S. M., & Stayton, D. J. (1971). Individual differences in the strange-situation behavior of one-year-olds. In H. R. Schaffer (Ed.), *The origins of human social relations* (pp. 17–52). Academic Press.
Ainsworth, M. D. S., Blehar, M. C., Waters, E., & Wall, S. (1978). *Patterns of attachment: A psychological study of the strange situation*. Lawrence Erlbaum.
Ainsworth, M., Boston, M., Bowlby, J., & Rosenbluth, D. (1956). The effects of mother-child separation: A follow-up study. *British Journal of Medical Psychology, 29*(3–4), 211–247.
Barba-Müller, E., Craddock, S., Carmona, S., & Hoekzema, E. (2019). Brain plasticity in pregnancy and the postpartum period: Links to maternal caregiving and mental health. *Archives of Women's Mental Health, 22*(2), 289–299. https://doi.org/10.1007/s00737-018-0889-z
Batstra, L., & Frances, A. (2025). Diagnosing the context is as important as diagnosing the individual. *Frontiers in Psychiatry, 16*, 1698878. https://doi.org/10.3389/fpsyt.2025.1698878
Beacon House Bruce Perry's Hierarchy of Brain Development. (2019). Retrieved May, 2025, from www.beaconhouse.org.uk
Beebe, B. (2017). Daniel Stern: Microanalysis and the empirical infant research foundations. *Psychoanalytic Inquiry, 37*(4), 228–241. https://doi.org/10.1080/07351690.2017.1299498
Berger, P. L., & Luckmann, T. (1966). *The social construction of reality: A treatise in the sociology of knowledge*. Doubleday & Company.
Bion, W. R. (1962). *Learning from experience*. Heinemann.
Boeree, C. G. (2006). *Personality theories*. http://webspace.ship.edu/cgboer/perscontents.html
Bowlby, J. (1944). Forty-four juvenile thieves: Their characters and home-life. *The International Journal of Psychoanalysis, 25*, 19–53.
Bowlby, J. (1951). Maternal care and mental health. *Bulletin of the World Health Organization, 3*, 355–533.
Bowlby, J. (1958). The nature of the child's tie to his mother. *The International Journal of Psychoanalysis, 39*, 350–373.
Bowlby, J. (1960a). Separation anxiety: A critical review of the literature. *The Journal of Child Psychology and Psychiatry, 1*(4), 251–269.
Bowlby, J. (1960b). Grief and mourning in infancy and early childhood. *Psychoanalytic Study of the Child, 15*, 9–52.

R. Swanick, *A Clinical Guide to Interpersonal Constructs and Attachment Theory*, https://doi.org/10.1007/978-3-032-23728-6

Bowlby, J. (1969). *Attachment and loss* (Vol. 1: Attachment). Basic Books.

Bowlby, J. ([1969] 1982). *Attachment*. Penguin.

Bowlby, J., Fry, M., & Ainsworth, M. D. S. (1953). *Child care and the growth of love*. Penguin Books.

Bretherton, I (1992). https://psychology.psy.sunysb.edu/attachment/online/inge_origins%20DP1992.pdf

Caldwell, L., & Robinson, H. T. (Eds.). (2017). *The collected works of D.W. Winnicott* (pp. 1–12). Oxford University Press.

Courchesne, E., Campbell, K., & Solso, S. (2011). Brain growth across the life span in autism: Age-specific changes in anatomical pathology. *Brain Research, 1380*, 138–145. https://doi.org/10.1016/j.brainres.2010.09.101

Craik, K. J. W. (1943). *The nature of explanation*. Cambridge University Press.

Crittenden, P. (1990). Internal representational models of attachment relationships. *Tradition - A Journal of Orthodox Jewish Thought., 11*, 259–277. https://doi.org/10.1002/1097-0355(199023)11:3<259::AID-IMHJ2280110308>3.0.CO;2-J

Crittenden, P. M. (2006). A dynamic-maturational model of attachment. *ANZJFT Australian and New Zealand Journal of Family Therapy, 27*(2), 105–115. https://doi.org/10.1002/j.1467-8438.2006.tb00704.x

Crittenden, P.M. (2015). Raising parents: Attachment, representation, and treatment.

Crittenden, P. M. (2017). Gifts from Mary Ainsworth and John Bowlby. *Clinical child Psychology and Psychiatry [Online], 22*(3), 436–442.

Crittenden, P. M., Lang, C., Claussen, A. H., & Partridge, M. F. (2000). Relations among mothers' dispositional representations of parenting. In P. M. Crittenden & A. H. Claussen (Eds.), *The organization of attachment relationships: Maturation, culture, and context* (pp. 214–233). Cambridge University Press.

de Silva, P. N. (2018). Do patterns of synaptic pruning underlie psychoses, autism and ADHD? *BJPsych Advances, 24*(3), 212–217. https://doi.org/10.1192/bja.2017.27

Duschinsky, R. (2024). Mary Main: Portrait and tribute. *Attachment & Human Development, 27*(1), 156–189. https://doi.org/10.1080/14616734.2024.2400808

Duschinsky, R. (2025). Epilogue. *Developments in Attachment Research*, 1 (Oxford, 2025; online edn, Oxford Academic, 2 June 2025). https://doi.org/10.1093/9780191976643.003.0006, Accessed 27 Dec. 2025.

Ezquerro, A. (2016). *Encounters with John Bowlby: Tales of attachment* (1st ed.). Routledge.

First 1000 Days of Life. Retrieved November, 2025, from https://publications.parliament.uk/pa/cm201719/cmselect/cmhealth/1496/1496.pdf.

Foucault, M. (1978). *The history of sexuality, Volume 1: An introduction* (page 86, translated by Robert Hurley).

Freud, S. (1912). The dynamics of transference. In *The standard edition of the complete psychological works of Sigmund Freud* (Vol. XII, pp. 97–108). Hogarth Press.

George, C., Kaplan, N., & Main, M. (1985). Attachment interview for adults.

Gilbert, P. (2024). Threat, safety, safeness and social safeness 30 years on: Fundamental dimensions and distinctions for mental health and well-being. *The British Journal of Clinical Psychology, 63*(3), 453–471. https://doi.org/10.1111/bjc.12466

Halbe, E., Schulze, M., Lux, S., Coghill, D., & Philipsen, A. (2025). Decision-making in attention-deficit/hyperactivity disorder (ADHD). In U. Ettinger, B. Heinrichs, & C. Murawski (Eds.), *Decision making. Studies in neuroscience, psychology and behavioral economics*. Springer. https://doi.org/10.1007/978-3-032-00880-0_15

Hinkle, D. (1965). *The change of personal constructs from the viewpoint of theory of construct implications*. Unpublished doctoral dissertation, Ohio State University.

Kaur, S., & Békés, V. (2025). The role of attachment in intergenerational trauma transmission: A structured literature review. *Journal of Aggression, Maltreatment & Trauma, 34*(10), 1560–1584. https://doi.org/10.1080/10926771.2025.2574315

Kelly, G. A. (1955). *The psychology of personal constructs* (Vol. 1 & 2). Norton.

Klein, M. (1946). Notes on some schizoid mechanisms. *International Journal of Psycho-Analysis, 27*, 99–110.

Landfield, A.W. (1971). Personal construct systems in psychotherapy.

Lieneman, C., Simpson, M., & McNeil, C. B. (2025). Bowlby, John. *Essays in Developmental Psychology, 30*. https://nsuworks.nova.edu/edp/30

Lorenz, K. Z. (1937). The companion in the bird's world. *The Auk, 54*(3), 245–273.

Lorenz, K. (1970). *Studies in animal and human behaviour* (Vol. 1). Harvard University Press.

Main, M., Kaplan, N., & Cassidy, J. (1985). Security in infancy, childhood, and adulthood: A move to the level of representation. *Monographs of the Society for Research in Child Development, 50*(1/2), 66–104. https://doi.org/10.2307/3333827

Main, M., & Solomon, J. (1986). Discovery of an insecure-disorganized/disoriented attachment pattern. In T. Brazelton et al. (Eds.), *Affective development in infancy*.

Main, M., & Solomon, J. (1990). Procedures for identifying infants as disorganized/disoriented during the Ainsworth strange situation. In M. T. Greenberg et al. (Eds.), *Attachment in pre-school years*.

Main, M., & Weston, D. R. (1981). The quality of the toddler's relationship to mother and to father: Related to conflict behavior and the readiness to establish new relationships. *Child Development*, 932–940. https://doi.org/10.2307/1129097

Maslow, A. H. (1943). A theory of human motivation. *Psychological Review, 50*(4), 370–396. https://doi.org/10.1037/h0054346

Mikulincer, M., & Shaver, P. (2003). The attachment behavioral system in adulthood: Activation, psychodynamics, and interpersonal processes. *Advances in Experimental Social Psychology, 35*, 53–152. https://doi.org/10.1016/S0065-2601(03)01002-5

Milton, D., Gurbuz, E., & López, B. (2022). The 'double empathy problem': Ten years on. *Autism, 26*(8), 1901–1903. https://doi.org/10.1177/13623613221129123. (Original work published 2022).

Mousley, A., Bethlehem, R. A. I., Yeh, F. C., & Astle, D. E. (2025). Topological turning points across the human lifespan. *Nature Communications, 16*(1), 10055. https://doi.org/10.1038/s41467-025-65974-8

National Institute of Mental Health, NIMH. (2007). Retreived February, 2026, from https://www.nimh.nih.gov/news/science-updates/2007/brain-matures-a-few-years-late-in-adhd-but-follows-normal-pattern

Papert, S. (1980). *Mindstorms: Children, computers, and powerful ideas*. Basic Books.

Pavlov, I. P. (1927). *Conditioned reflexes: An investigation of the physiological activity of the cerebral cortex*. Oxford University Press.

Perry, B. D. (2006). Applying principles of neurodevelopment to clinical work with maltreated and traumatized children: The neurosequential model of therapeutics. In N. B. Webb (Ed.), *Working with traumatized youth in child welfare* (pp. 27–52). The Guilford Press.

Perry, B. D. (2009). Examining child maltreatment through a neurodevelopmental lens: Clinical applications of the neurosequential model of therapeutics. *Journal of Loss and Trauma, 14*(4), 240–255.

Perry, B. D., & Szalavitz, M. (2006). The boy who was raised as a dog: And other stories from a child psychiatrist's notebook.

Piaget, J. (1936). *La naissance de l'intelligence chez l'enfant*. Delachaux et Niestlé.

Piaget, J. (1952). *The origins of intelligence in children*. International Universities Press.

Piaget, J. (1964). Cognitive development in children: Development and learning. *Journal of Research in Science Teaching, 2*, 176–186. https://doi.org/10.1002/tea.3660020306

Porges, S. W. (2022). Polyvagal theory: A science of safety. *Frontiers in Integrative Neuroscience, 16*, 871227. https://doi.org/10.3389/fnint.2022.871227

Procter, H. (1985). A construct approach to family therapy and systems intervention. In E. Button (Ed.), *Personal construct theory and mental health*. Croom Helm.

Procter, H. (2017, August). Chapter six: Family constructs and semantic polarities: A convergent perspective. In *Personal construct psychology at 60: Papers from the 21st international congress* (p. 68). Cambridge Scholars Publishing.

Procter, H. (2022). Procter H G PhD Thesis PCT and the Family - A Theoretical and Methodological Study 1978–2022.

Quinn, H. (2019). Jean Piaget and Lev Vygotsky. *Indiana South Bend University: Undergraduate Research Journal.*

Stern, W. (1912). *Die psychologischen Methoden der Intelligenzprüfung und ihre Anwendung an Schulkindern* [The psychological methods of testing intelligence]. Barth.

Stern, D. (1985). *The interpersonal world of the infant.* Basic Books.

Stern, D. N. (2010). *Forms of vitality: Exploring dynamic experience in psychology, the arts, psychotherapy, and development.* Oxford University Press.

Stevenson-Hinde, J. (2007). Attachment theory and John Bowlby: Some reflections. *Attachment & Human Development, 9*(4), 337–342.

Terman, L. M. (1916). *The measurement of intelligence.* Houghton Mifflin.

Ugazio, V., & Dixon, R. (2013). Semantic polarities and psychopathologies in the family: Permitted and forbidden stories. *Semantic Polarities and Psychopathologies in the Family: Permitted and Forbidden Stories*, 1–327. https://doi.org/10.4324/9780203552384

van der Horst, F. C., & van der Veer, R. (2009). Separation and divergence: The untold story of James Robertson's and John Bowlby's theoretical dispute on mother-child separation. *Journal of the History of the Behavioral Sciences, 45*(3), 236–252. https://doi.org/10.1002/jhbs.20380

Van IJzendoorn, M. H., & Bakermans-Kranenburg, M. J. (1997). Intergenerational transmission of attachment. A move to the contextual level. In L. Atkinson & K. J. Zucker (Eds.), *Attachment and psychopathology* (pp. 135–170).

Vicedo, M. (2011). The social nature of the mother's tie to her child: John Bowlby's theory of attachment in post-war America. *The British Journal for the History of Science, 44*(3), 401–426. http://www.jstor.org/stable/41241684

Vygotsky, L. S. (1978). *Mind in society: The development of higher psychological processes.* Harvard University Press.

Winnicott, D. W. (1953). Transitional objects and transitional phenomena; a study of the first not-me possession. *The International Journal of Psychoanalysis, 34*, 89–97.

Winnicott, D. W. (1956). Primary maternal preoccupation. In *Through paediatrics to psycho-analysis: Collected papers* (pp. 300–305). Tavistock.

Winnicott, D. W. (1965). *The maturational processes and the facilitating environment: Studies in the theory of emotional development.*

Winnicott, D. W. (2005). *Playing and reality* (2nd ed.). Routledge.

Wood, D., Bruner, J. S., & Ross, G. (1976). The role of tutoring in problem solving. *Journal of Child Psychology and Psychiatry, 17*(2), 89–100.

Yalom, I. (2009). *The gift of therapy.* HarperCollins.

Yanpei, W., Chenyi, Z., Qinfang, X., Lei, H., & Yuning, Z. (2021). Attention-deficit/hyperactivity disorder is characterized by a delay in subcortical maturation. *Progress in Neuro-Psychopharmacology and Biological Psychiatry, 104*, 110044.

Zaccagnino, M., Cussino, M., Saunders, R., Jacobvitz, D., & Veglia, F. (2014). Alternative caregiving figures and their role on adult attachment representations. *Clinical Psychology & Psychotherapy, 21*(3), 276–287. https://doi.org/10.1002/cpp.1828

Index

R. Swanick, *A Clinical Guide to Interpersonal Constructs and Attachment Theory*, https://doi.org/10.1007/978-3-032-23728-6

MIX
Papier aus verantwortungsvollen Quellen
Paper from responsible sources
FSC® C105338
FSC
www.fsc.org

If you have any concerns about our products,
you can contact us on
ProductSafety@springernature.com

In case Publisher is established outside the EU,
the EU authorized representative is:
Springer Nature Customer Service Center GmbH
Europaplatz 3, 69115 Heidelberg, Germany

Printed by Libri Plureos GmbH
in Hamburg, Germany